LIGHTS AND SHADOWS
OF
THE SACRED MINISTRY

BY THE REVEREND

ARCHIBALD CAMPBELL KNOWLES, D.D.

RECTOR OF SAINT ALBAN'S CHURCH,
OLNEY, PHILADELPHIA

And Author of "The Practice of Religion"
"The Life of Offering," "The Holy Christ Child,"
"The Triumph of the Cross," "Adventures in the Alps,"
"Reminiscences of a Parish Priest"
"A Rendezvous with Destiny," Etc.

"First, give thyself to God:
Then to the work God gives thee to do."
(Saint Augustine)

WEST PARK, N. Y.

HOLY CROSS PRESS

1947

111940

COPYRIGHT, 1947

ARCHIBALD CAMPBELL KNOWLES

TO
THE GLORY OF GOD
AND
IN HONOUR OF
OUR BLESSED LORD
IN WHOSE NAME
EVERY PRIEST DOTH MINISTER

"Give me the Priest, a Light upon a Hill,
Whose Rays his whole Circumference can fill;
In God's Own Word, and sacred Learning versed,
Deep in the Study of the Heart immersed,
Who in such Souls can the Disease descry,
And wisely fit Restoratives apply.
Give me the Priest these graces shall possess—
Of an Ambassador the first address;
A Father's tenderness, a Shepherd's care;
A Leader's courage, who the Cross can bear;
A Ruler's awe, a Watchman's wakeful eye;
A Pilot's skill, the helm in storms to ply;
A Fisher's patience, a Labourer's toil;
A Guide's dexterity to disembroil;
A Prophet's inspiration from above;
A Teacher's knowledge and a Saviour's love."

PREFACE

BY THE BISHOP OF MILWAUKEE

It has been a pleasure and a privilege for me to read the manuscript of this book by the Reverend Archibald Campbell Knowles, whom I have known these many years.

I thank God that He has inspired His servant to write this little book, a simple setting forth of the life, responsibilities and the rule of life of the Priest. It might also prove profitable reading for the Laity, that they might have a helpful understanding of the ideals and principles of their Pastors, and lead to a happy cooperation of Priest and People.

We priests do so need an ordered life. We all of us have some Rule of Life, but seldom is the Rule an adequate one for those who are constantly seeking to be the best and most worthy Priests and Pastors. The pressure of secular things, and the details of Pastoral work tend to make us careless in our inner lives and so we often fail to see our Ministry as a whole.

Dr. Knowles has done all of us in Holy Orders a helpful service in this presentation of the joys, blessings and responsibilities of the Sacred Ministry. He speaks out of a rich and devoted service of more than forty years in this Ministry.

Dr. Knowles is a devoted Priest, an indefatigable Pastor and a wise counsellor. In this book he speaks out of a long experience with sympathy and understanding. It is given to very few to have experienced such a ministry as his has been. Under his leadership, his congregation has developed from a tiny Mission to a strong Parish and he has consistently taught and practiced the full revelation of God and the traditions of the Catholic Church.

It would be helpful for all of us to re-read this little work at least once a year, perhaps in connection with a Retreat, to recall us to our ideals, and to stimulate us to higher ones. If every Aspirant for Holy Orders could read this book and if every young Priest could have a copy and for at least the first five years of his ministry re-read it occasionally, they would be much profited. Those of the Laity might also find it most advantageous to read.

May God bless this helpful work as God has blessed Father Knowles's long and fruitful ministry.

BENJAMIN F. P. IVINS,

Bishop of Milwaukee.

FOREWORD

BY THE BISHOP OF PENNSYLVANIA

A FAVORITE ATTITUDE for many in matters of religion is sitting on the fence. They do not want to come down on one side or the other. Father Knowles comes down hard on the Anglo-Catholic side. As a matter of fact, he has never been on the fence! His life has been and is a sincere endeavor to practice what he advocates so positively in this book. He knows that I do not agree with all of his conclusions, but I am very happy to recommend this book for reading to the clergy and laity generally as being very helpful.

OLIVER J. HART,

Bishop of Pennsylvania.

PREFACE BY THE AUTHOR

THIS LITTLE BOOK has been written: to attract to the Sacred Ministry those religiously inclined, including those returning from the war; to impress upon all of the Clergy the joys, blessings privileges and responsibilities of the clerical life; and to try to inspire all to a more devoted love of the things of God. And if many of the Laity read, as is hoped, that they may have a better understanding of the high office of a Priest and be more loyal and loving to his authority and counsel.

It has seemed expedient briefly to touch upon the Church, the Scriptures and the Sacraments and certain teachings that those considering a "call" to the Sacred Ministry may better appreciate the True Religion and have as it were a realistic background. And it may be that these special chapters may also be of value to those of us who have long been in Holy Orders.

The Author does not presume to give any instruction or counsel to his brethren, except as it applies to us all, the aim being rather that we may all more clearly realize our blessings and responsibilities, more faithfully discharge our duties, and try to live up to the high ideals and standards set forth. For while it is true that many will probably fall short of this, it is also true that we will be better men and Priests if we keep such ideals and standards before us and strive to attain unto them.

It may be noticed that there is an occasional repetition of certain thoughts and texts, especially regarding the Church and the Sacraments. This has been intentional, in the desire to stress certain things and to make each chapter complete in itself. In themes so closely related, it was difficult not to do this without hurting the context.

No one is more conscious than the Author of his failing to do full justice to the great subject of the Sacred Ministry. Yet it is his hope that God will accept his humble endeavor to advance the cause of Christ and the Church, blessing all that is good, forgiving all that is imperfect, and making all redound to His Honour and Glory.

CONTENTS

"Thou art a place to hide me in."

"JESU, grant me this, I pray,
Ever in Thy Heart to stay;
Let me evermore abide
Hidden in Thy wounded Side.

If the evil one prepare,
Or the world, a tempting snare,
I am safe when I abide
In Thy Heart and wounded Side.

If the flesh, more dangerous still,
Tempt my soul to deeds of ill,
Nought I fear when I abide
In Thy Heart and wounded Side.

Death will come one day to me;
JESU, cast me not from Thee:
Dying let me still abide
In Thy Heart and wounded Side."

I

A GLORIOUS HERITAGE

As one approaches the consideration of the Sacred Ministry, how is it written large in the pages of history! How intimately is it connected with Art, Architecture, Music and Literature! As the pages of history for two thousand years come before our eyes, how they picture many in Holy Orders, whose character, writing or deeds made them shining lights for all time. How many of them were Saints, forever enrolled in that "multitude which none can number," whose lives were lived entirely for the Glory of God. What they were and what they did not only affected their own day, but also have their influence upon the present age. Throughout the Christian centuries we see the Clergy, not only ministering the Word and the Sacraments and carrying the Gospel far and wide, but also acting as the preservers of learning, the builders of Churches, the cultivators of the Arts, the advocates of justice, law and order, the protectors of the poor and the opponents of tyranny and oppression. And being human, the fact of shadows sometimes mingling with the lights, and occasionally some of the Clergy, especially those in high place, being evil doers, only serves by contrast to make still more glorious the lives of the far greater number who faithfully served their Divine

1

Master and lived and died "in the odour of Sanctity."

Long is the list of those in the Sacred Ministry whose memory lives today as great Saints, Scholars, Theologians, Philosophers, humanitarians and men of God. Space would not permit even a scanty notice of the vast throng, not only of those who glorified the page of history and whose praises are still sung by the Church, and the world, but also of those who, born to a more humble lot, "to fortune and to fame unknown," were an inspiration and a benediction to all who met them in the way. Yet a few, a very few, chosen almost at random, may be mentioned, as illustrating certain periods in which they stand out as high lights.

What wonderful men were the Apostles! Chosen by Christ, mostly unlearned men, from ordinary walks of life, how through the teaching of Our Lord and the illumination of the Holy Ghost, they become the greatest of all missionaries and martyrs! And their immediate followers, how history and tradition points to them as the great leaders of the host to come. One pictures Saint John carried about the streets of Ephesus preaching the love of God; of Saint Paul on Mar's Hill at Athens before the Altar "of the unknown God," revealing the True Religion; of Saint Peter in his prison at Rome; of Saint Luke painting the Nativity and preaching of the Holy Christ Child! All of these are the forerunners of men in the Sacred Ministry today leaving "their footprints in the sands of time."

And what majestic figures stand out through these Christian Ages! Saint Athanasius "against the world," defending "the Faith once for all delivered to the Saints"; Saint Augustine, turning from paganism, to be one of the greatest Bishops of the Church; Saint Ambrose on the steps of the Cathedral of Milan reproving the Emperor and forbidding entrance except upon repentance; Saint Benedict, forsaking the world and laying the foundation of the Rule for the Monastic Life that is followed in the main by all the Religious today; Pope Leo, the Great, in cope and mitre and surrounded by his Clergy, saving Rome from Attila and the Huns; Saint Patrick taking the Christian Religion to Ireland, to make the land known far and wide as "the Isle of the Saints"—one could go on and on, and yet those named would only be a few of the many just as notable!

Or, turning to mediaeval times, how the Church rejoices and those in the Sacred Ministry are inspired over such names as the Venerable Bede, almost to his last moments translating the Scriptures so dearly loved; Saint Thomas Aquinas, called the "Angelic Doctor," the greatest Theologian of all time and whose eucharistic hymns are amongst today's treasures of worship; Saint Bernard, preaching the Crusades and founding the famous Cistercian Monastery in the midst of the forests of Clairvaux; of Thomas à Kempis, kneeling in his cell, writing "The Imitation of Christ"; of Stephen Langton, Archbishop of Canterbury, leading the Nobles to obtain the "Magna Charta" of the liberties of the people, the groundwork of Democracy today:—here again the omissions far outnumber the names included.

One looks at the Cathedrals as at Nôtre Dame, Paris, and here is the work of those in Holy Order. Or at the ruined Abbeys, as Fountains, Glastonbury or Tinterne, England, and one sees the work of the

Clergy. Or at some of the most loved works of art, and Fra Angelico, Fra Filippo Lippi and others show how many monks were artists, painting pictures and illuminating manuscripts. And passing on, still at random, one thinks of Savanarola, burnt at the stake because of his reforms; Bossuet, a holy Bishop in an evil age, who, amongst other things, wrote his book on the Sermon on the Mount; Saint Vincent de Paul, the great French Reformer of the 17th century, founding his many charities and especially for the care of children; Saint Francis de Sales, whose devotional books today are in many households; Father Marquette in Canada and elsewhere carrying the Christian Religion to the Indians; Father Damien bringing the Church and the Sacraments and hope to the poor stricken lepers of the Sandwich Islands;— all of these our inheritance in the Sacred Ministry.

The Church of England at home and in her Colonies and the Episcopal Church in America and in her missionary districts can point with pride to the many who, in comparatively modern times and today, have carried on the glorious traditions of the Ministry in the past. Their names are legion. They are not confined to any party. They are not from any special class. They represent "all sorts and conditions of men," and show that even today, in far easier times, there can be true consecration, real heroism and holy living that make the Clergy stand out amongst their brethren as true leaders and fine examples. Perhaps the Anglo-Catholic Revival gives as good a picture as any, in Dr. Pusey, Canon Carter, John Keble, John Mason Neale, Canon Liddon, Father Mackonochie, Father Stanton, Bishop King, Canon Knox-Little, and Bishop Weston, and those splendid Priests who one time ministered in the slums of London and Portsmouth, Father Wilson and Father Dolling. Here in this group, chosen at random, is seen notable writing in poetry and prose, theological learning of the highest order and consecrated lives that may be an inspiration to all.

And the present, as the past, also has its great names, but it is better, perhaps, not to mention personally those who are in our midst today, or who have but recently passed on. For all the decline and neglect of religion in the past fifty years (a decline and neglect it is hoped will disappear at the end of this great war) there have been many in the Sacred Ministry, both here and abroad, who have well lived up to the ideals and traditions of the days gone by. And again, it is not confined to any party, place or class. The early history of the Anglican Communion in America shows many splendid soldiers and servants of Christ and today in many diverse and varied places, Bishops and Priests are standing out boldly for the Faith, are diligently ministering the Word and the Sacraments and are living truly consecrated and self-sacrificing lives. So our heritage in the Sacred Ministry is one to cherish and value, is one to attract others to follow on in their steps, is one to make all try to measure up!

From this rather rambling resume of the Christian Era, it is seen how prominent has been the position and the influence of the Church and the Clergy. And it is coming to be more and more realized that the world will be better and happier the more this religious leadership is restored and an inspiring ideal held up by "the Man of God." For the upheaval of the Reformation and the consequent injury to the unity of Christendom is responsible for many of the evils of the last three hundred years.

Yet still the Church does, at times, speak with authority, as in the Anglican Communion through such great leaders as the Archbishop of Canterbury and the Bishops of London and New York and others, and in the Roman Catholic body in a stronger way through the Holy Father at Rome, whose words have binding force on the many millions of his followers. Through the Anglican Communion and through the Roman Catholic body it is the Holy Catholic Church speaking, and although separated outwardly by certain differences, they may speak as one on many social, moral and religious matters and put all the power and influence of the Church on the side of righteousness and justice.

Here then in the Sacred Ministry is a great opportunity for the young adventurous spirit capable of visualizing the glorious privilege of serving God in this way, of following Christ in winning souls, in spreading the Kingdom of Heaven. The Church is a glorious heritage. The Priesthood is an exalted office. The work is a splendid chance. What joy, what happiness, what triumph awaits those who, accepting such Service, taking up such responsibilities, consecrate their time and talents to the most glorious field of labour for Christ and the Church. To many of you who read, God may be calling, to follow these great lights in a world darkened by sin!

II

THE DIVINE CALL

OUR BLESSED LORD and Saviour founded the Church, preached the gospel, revealed the Faith once for all delivered to the Saints, instituted the Sacraments and chose the Apostles as the Sacred Ministry.

This Sacred Ministry has come down throughout the centuries through that which is known as the Apostolic Succession. This is the descent through Episcopal Ordination, it being necessary to a valid ministry to receive the "Laying on of hands" by a Bishop, in full communion with the Holy Catholic Church. The greatest care has been taken in this, every precaution and safeguard being used to prevent any defect in this Ministry. There has always been the insistence upon valid "form," "matter" and "intention." Thus the same powers and privileges as were conferred upon the first followers of Our Lord are received by Priests today, ordained in the Holy Catholic Church, their commission coming from Christ, their authority from His Church.

One comes to the Sacred Ministry in a different way from that followed in entering most other careers. With most walks of life, it is a *"choice."* With the Sacred Ministry it is a *"call."* It is the difference between a *"profession"* and a *"vocation."*

For it is always assumed that those entering upon the Sacred Priesthood are called by God to that office.

This does not mean that "the call" always comes in the same way or is always so clear as to be at once recognized. Some will hear *"the Still Small Voice"* and feel that Christ is as truly calling them as He called His Apostles, that they must drop everything and follow Him. This, if real, should be a very blessed experience, and fortunate are those who have such a call.

Many others, however, are led on indirectly, little by little, realizing that Our Lord is showing them the way through their experiences in life, such as a great absorbing love of Souls, a strong liking for all things connected with the Church, a special bent for things of a religious or spiritual nature, a gift for influencing those about one, or the conviction that one's talents are specially suited to the Ministry and can best be exercised in the things of God. To all intents and purposes any of these constitutes a "call," although there may be great heart searchings before such call becomes clear, convincing and imperative.

God's ways *"are wonderful and past finding out,"* but His Will is always accomplished. Old and young are called to serve Christ in the Sacred Ministry. Some start their career in that Holy Office, others come to it after many years spent in other fields of labour. Some dedicate themselves early to God, others come to Him after a brilliant record in the world. The drawing power of Christ is ever the same. Both the world and the Church are richer for the one who forsakes the world for the Church.

The call to the Sacred Ministry (except in the case of "the Religious," who take upon themselves special vows of Poverty, Chastity and Obedience) does not necessarily mean the change of one's mode of life, where it is lived according to the commandments of God, and where it does not conflict with one's ministerial duties. If one has social position and large financial means, they can be specially used in the Sacred Ministry for God's Glory. So with teaching talent, or literary ability, or artistic, architectural or musical gifts. In the present as in the past, they can be best exercised in the work of the Church. The world abounds with the accomplishments of the Clergy in all these ways, illuminating with light the pages of history and civilization.

On the other hand, those who are full of the spirit of sacrifice, and see in this a closer union with Christ, will best find the way of realization of this in the Sacred Ministry of the Church. There are the countless opportunities: the ascetic life that shows renunciation of much that the world considers necessary, the unnoticed "Cure" in some humble parish, the devoted service given in the drab and dingy environment of the slum, the glorious missionary labours in some foreign land that knows not God. All of these and many other opportunities offer themselves to those who would in the most literal sense take up their Cross daily and follow Christ.

The Church in its Ordination Service seeks to uphold the highest ideal and standard of the Sacred Ministry and aims to prevent anyone seeking this holy office from unworthy motives. No one should enter upon this calling from a desire for place or preferment, or to promote one's social status, or to follow an easier way of living, which is here possible to those who shut their eyes to the call of duty. The sole motive should be to serve in the Sacred Ministry for the Glory of God, devotion to Christ and the love of Souls, to dedicate one's God-given talents to God's special work in the Church.

The Church desires a learned Clergy but above all a consecrated Clergy. Throughout one's whole life in the Sacred Ministry, so far as possible, a certain time should be given to study; chiefly, of course, in the things of God, although all real culture is a help in any work. Some who hear "the Divine Call" will go to the Theological Seminaries. Some will study privately with tutors, under the Bishop. Generally speaking, it is considered advisable that the candidate for Holy Orders has had the benefit of an University or College education or its equivalent, and has a fair knowledge of Latin and Greek, even if Hebrew is dispensed with as is often the case.

In considering the "call" to Holy Orders, some hesitate, for fear that they will not be able properly to fulfill their vows. While this is commendable, if it comes from humility, it is mistaken if it arises from a lack of trust. For we must ever remember, that as the Ordination Service clearly states, we cannot do these things by our own power but only through the grace of God. Our Lord said *"My grace is sufficient for thee."* This grace is always forthcoming to that soul which casts all his care upon God. It never fails but is there in every need in response to prayer and sacrament. As one does not hesitate about Confirmation or Marriage Vows, so one should not doubt about Ordination Vows. One might be counselled: *"The Eternal God is thy refuge: Underneath are the Everlasting Arms,"* for

God in Christ is ever sustaining those who try to be faithful in the Sacred Ministry.

To one with a real "Call" the work of the Sacred Ministry is never drab or dull but is ever of absorbing interest and increasingly attractive. It is really a great "adventure for God." As a soldier in a battle, as a pioneer in the wilderness, as a sailor in a storm, as a climber on a mountain, the very difficulties and danger add joy and zest to the efforts. It is worth while to wage war with the world, the flesh and the devil, to seek to make the wilderness of the earth the garden of God, to try to win through midst the troubled seas of sin and ignorance to the haven of God, to seek those spiritual heights from which the splendor of God is revealed, to do all this and win out! Yet each one called must give himself up unreservedly, offer himself in full surrender and consecration to God. Thus only will he be able to go forward with a smile on his face, and determination in his heart, from *"strength to strength"* and *"from grace to grace,"* as he humbly uses all of his talents and abilities, always conscious that he can only succeed through the help of God.

One very essential thing to success in this work is that the Priest should be an optimist, with a smile on his face and determination in his heart, in all that he does, bringing a joy both to himself and to those amongst whom he works. To the Faith, Hope and Charity, in which virtues he tries consistently and conscientiously to practice his religion, should be added courage, patience and perseverance, and the ever trying to maintain a balanced judgment, a sense of proportion and the gift of humour.

No one really worth while ever desires to find all things easy, for nothing worth having or doing can be had except through consecrated work and effort, with the consequent joy of overcoming difficulties and surmounting impediments. So with the Sacred Ministry, it is no easy road, but quite the contrary, with its many trials, disappointments, problems and the constant round of duty. Yet to one truly called, to one fully consecrated, the winning out will be an incentive inspiring to a degree and the lights will overwhelm the shadows and the successes will outweigh the failures, the joys will conquer the sorrows, and there will be a happiness, a peace, a satisfaction such as can be obtained in no other walk of life.

Today the Church offers an unusual opportunity to men of vision to enlist as soldiers and servants of Christ in the Sacred Ministry. To devote oneself heart and soul to *"the things of God"* is worthy of the ablest men. For rightly understood, the office of a Priest is one entitled to the greatest honour, in which one exercises the ministry of our Blessed Lord and treads in the footsteps of some of the greatest lights of the world. While *"all sorts and conditions of men"* should have access to this Sacred Office, and if qualified be ordained to serve the Lord Christ in this way, it is nevertheless desirable that men of birth and position, of education and culture, should offer themselves for this high calling. And amongst those returning from the war, surely there will be many who will wish to serve God in the Ministry as they have served the nation in its Army and Navy. No other calling gives such great opportunity of making reparation to God for the great sins committed against Him by nations and individuals. The Ministry gives the privilege of offering *"vicarious sacrifice"* for the souls of others.

III

THE HOLY CATHOLIC CHURCH

IN ENTERING the Sacred Ministry, one is not being ordained in a man-made organization but in a Divine Institution, the Holy Catholic Church, which was instituted and commissioned by Our Lord Jesus Christ. It is His Mystical Body, embracing the Living and the Dead; that is "the Church Militant," "the Church Expectant," and "the Church Triumphant." The purpose of the Church is to set forth the Christian Religion, to minister the Word and the Sacraments and to bring Souls into union with God. The Church is guided by the Holy Ghost, speaks with Divine Authority and is the Preserver of Truth, the Dispenser of Grace and the Guide in Morals. She teaches that which is right as to Doctrine, Discipline and Worship, and her authorty and not private judgment is the sole judge as to Faith and Practice. This has clearly been set forth in the Creeds, the Scriptures, the Liturgies, the Councils and Canons of the Church and is known as *"The Faith once for all delivered to the Saints."* It is the duty of all to submit to the authority of the Church and to conform to her godly commands and counsels.

Our Blessed Lord only preached *one* Religion and only instituted *one* Church. For centuries this was everywhere acknowledged and those disputing the authority of the Church or teaching false doctrine were regarded as heretics and schismatics.

To preserve inviolate the Doctrine, Discipline and Worship of the Church, and especially to define the true belief as to the Person and Natures of Our Lord, from time to time Councils were called. Those admitted to be General or Æcumenical Councils (that is at which the whole Church was represented and the decrees universally accepted) are generally accounted to be seven: Nicaea 325 A.D., Constantinople 381, Ephesus 434, Chalcedon 451, Constantinople 553, Constantinople 680 and Nicaea 787. One result was the putting forth of the Nicene Creed, largely through the efforts of Saint Athanasius, whose views later were summed up in the Creed that bears his name, (although probably written by Saint Hilary of Poictiers).

Those days were the times of the Apostolic Fathers and Ancient Doctors, the greatest of these being, amongst the Easterns or Greeks, Saint Athanasius, Saint Basil, Saint Chrysostom and Saint Gregory of Nazianzum, and amongst the Westerns or Latins, Saint Ambrose, Saint Augustine, Saint Jerome and Saint Leo.

In the early Church were five great Bishoprics or Patriarchates: Alexandria, Antioch, Constantinople, Jerusalem and Rome. About the fourth century Rome began to assume special prominence and to put forth claims of precedence, this aim and desire being greatly helped by the fall of the western part of the Roman Empire. The Papacy stressed the words: "Thou art Peter: upon this Rock I will built My Church," and while the majority of the Fathers and Theologians did not accept Rome's interpretation, gradually her primacy was more or less accepted by the whole western Church, although regarded by many as unscriptural and unhistorical.

In the 11th century came the first real break in the Church, due to the rivalry of the Bishops of Rome and Constantinople, the "Image Controversy" and the dispute about "the Procession of the Holy Ghost." This resulted in the separation of the Eastern and Western parts of the Church, which continues today.

During Mediaeval Times, great waves of good and evil successively swept over the Church. There were the so called "Dark Ages," when all kinds of superstition, corruption and scandalous living stained the pages of history. And there were the "Glorious Days," when the great Cathedrals were built, the Monastic Orders spread, the Preaching Friars came into being, the great universities arose, Art, Architecture, Music and Learning flourished, and Gothic Architecture with its beauty, majesty and aspiration witnessed to the True Faith and symbolized the devotion and religion of those times. In some ways the 13th century was the most inspiring and glorious of the whole Christian Era. Two dark spots were the Crusades, which starting in a noble motive brought in many corruptions, and the Black Death which devastated a large part of Europe.

In the 16th century came the so called Reformation, breaking the unity of the Western Church. It was started on the Continent by Martin Luther, an Augustinian Monk, who, rightly scandalized by the issue and sale of Indulgences, unfortunately opposed them in a way that caused his condemnation by the Council of Speyer. He and his followers protested, thus becoming the first "Protestants." It is one of the sad facts of history, that a well intentioned attempt to condemn an evil and to effect a reform resulted in Martin Luther being forced to leave the True Church and found his Lutheran Body. This paved the way for the innumerable Sects of the present day, and at the time led to catastrophe, persecution and war.

In England there also came the Reformation but in a very different way. There it was begun and carried on by the authorities of the Church of England, where, while renouncing allegiance to the Papacy, (asserting that the Bishop of Rome had no more right to jurisdiction over the Church of England than had any foreign Bishop) it *did not break* with the ancient Catholic Church but was *the same body* before and after the Reformation.

The Church of England was extended throughout the British possessions and Colonies. In America its followers were under the jurisdiction of the Bishop of London. When the War of Independence was ended, Churchmen organized an autonymous body, popularly called "the Episcopal Church," Dr. Seabury, the first Bishop being consecrated by the Episcopal Church of Scotland, and later Bishop White, Bishop Prevoost and Bishop Madison, receiving their consecration at the hands of the Archbishop of Canterbury and other Prelates of the Church of England. Sure of the Apostolic Succession, the Church in America has grown to be a large and prominent body, including "all sorts and conditions of men," and noted for its missionary work. Its influence is far beyond its position numerically. It is in communion with the Church of England and all other parts of the Anglican body.

The Christian world today presents the following picture: the One, Holy, Catholic and Apostolic Church, the Divine Institution of Our Lord, unfortunately divided into three great parts: the Anglican, the Eastern and Roman Communions. Outside the Church proper are over two hundred Sectarian bodies, who reject the authority of the Church and more or less follow false doctrine, heresy or schism, teaching for doctrine *"the commandment of men."* In many cases they show good lives and abound in good works. Those however holding the True Faith, as shown forth by the Holy Catholic Church will be humbly thankful that they have the assurance of the full measure of blessing which comes from the true Religion given by Our Lord: *"the Faith once for all delivered to the Saints."*

IV

THE ANGLICAN COMMUNION

THOSE FOR WHOM this book is written will naturally seek the Priesthood of the Anglican Communion. For to all practical intents and purposes the Holy Orthodox Eastern Church is to us a foreign body, with traditions, customs and ceremonial definitely Eastern. And speaking generally, the Roman Catholic body largely consists of the Latin peoples, the Irish and those of Irish descent and such others as own the Papal obedience. To those not of the east or not of Roman Catholic parentage, the Anglican Communion, with its services in "a tongue understanded of the people," and carrying on the glorious traditions of the Church of England will have a great appeal.

The Anglican Communion is a true part of the true Church. This is not a matter of opinion but a matter of fact. It has a valid Ministry, sure of the Apostolic Succession, in which, according to the ancient way, it is guided and governed by the collective Episcopate and not by one Bishop as in the Roman Catholic obedience. It has valid Sacraments, seven in number, with proper matter, form and intention, to make them vital powers for conferring grace, as they purport to be. And it has all that goes with the true Religion: the historic Creeds, the inspired Scriptures, the ancient traditions, and the Rites and Ceremonies hallowed by the use of centuries, or which have rightly developed from the original. Consequently the Anglican Communion should command and receive the undivided love and loyalty of all its members.

This Faith was taken to Britain in the first century. There the Church grew and flourished and was represented at early Councils. The British Church continued to hold and practice the ancient and Apostolic Faith, even when the land was conquered and overrun by the Angles, Saxons and Danes. And later, after the coming of Augustine, (who, assisted by the Scotch-Irish Monks from the North, converted these heathen newcomers), the British Christians were amalgamated with the others, as "the Church of England."

The coming of William the Conqueror brought still another strain into the Church. Those who love to seek origins and to trace causes may find much to study in this fusion of British, Angles, Saxons, Danes, Italians and Norman-French, which made the Church of England, as it were "sui generis," and characteristically repeatedly asserting its independent spirit, especially regarding the nominal jurisdiction of Rome, so that which was "implicit" in the earlier days, became "explicit" at the Reformation.

The Reformation in England was quite different from that on the Continent. It was done by the Church itself. It gave up nothing of Apostolic Faith and Practice. It retained the Ministry, the Word and the Sacraments in their integrity. It repudiated the Papal jurisdiction. It did away with superstitions, corruptions and abuses. It shortened, simplified, yet enriched the Services.

It is true that some mistakes were made, that occasional compromises took place, in order to hold the allegiance of all, that certain things were dropped which have only recently been restored by the Anglo-Catholic Revival, but as a whole the English Reformation was well done, as a needed purification of the Church. And in the succeeding centuries, for all the oft-time conflict between good and evil, throughout all the drift and deadness of morals and religion, through all the lights and shadows of the spiritual life, the Anglicans have preserved the True Religion, the revelation of Our Blessed Lord.

Those in the Anglican Communion, and especially those in the Sacred Priesthood, who minister at her Altars should be devoutly thankful for this great heritage from the past. They should also realize their solemn responsibility to do their part to hold and teach *"the Truth, the whole Truth and nothing but the Truth"* as loyal Anglicans, showing forth Catholic Faith and Practice, neither Roman nor Protestant, but in its apostolic purity, developed as it came down through the centuries. It is sometimes said that the Anglican Communion has a Catholic Clergy and a Protestant People. If there is truth in this, it is all the more the duty and the privilege of those in the Sacred Ministry to see that those in their charge are properly instructed in the Doctrine, Discipline and Worship of the Church.

The claim of the Anglican Communion to be a real part of the true Church does not have to be approved of Rome, for being a matter of fact, the Papal opinion cannot disprove it. It may well be remembered, however, that at the Reformation, the Pope offered to accede to all that had been done by the Church of England, if it would return to his jurisdiction. And the validity of Anglican Orders has repeatedly been admitted, as by Bishop Bossuet, Gasparri, Duchesne and the Sorbonne. It is not necessary for the Papacy to approve. Facts speak for themselves and the Anglican Communion is sure of her facts: that she is part of the Holy Catholic Church, with valid Ministry and Sacraments. It is *not* union with Rome that makes a Catholic! Nor is one a Catholic because he copies Rome and longs for her jurisdiction! Rome holds the Faith, is full of good works, is the larger part of the Church, but the Holy Father and his followers are unmistakably *Roman* Catholics, and by their own admission as witnessed in one of their Creeds are members of the *Holy Roman Church*.

Our Formularies and Traditions are Catholic, for all they are capable of improvement and enrichment. We own the authority of the Holy Catholic Church, in existence before the Papacy rose to power. We accept the Church as the Divine Institution of Christ, embracing the Living and the Dead. We have the Creeds, the Scriptures, the Sacraments, the ancient ministry of Bishops, Priests and Deacons, continued through the Apostolic Succession. We plead the Sacrifice of the Altar for the Living and the Dead and worship Our Lord Really, Spiritually and Objectively Present in the Blessed Sacrament. We preach the Gospel as the Church has received the same. We confess our sins and are absolved by the Priest acting in the Sacred Ministry as the accredited agent of Christ. We hold and hand down the Traditions of the Church as representing the human understanding of the Mind of God. We express and enshrine our worship in the beautiful and dignified Ceremonial hallowed by the use of centuries, or added to by a living body guided by God the Holy Ghost.

This is our heritage of Doctrine, Discipline and Worshp. *This is that which stamps the Anglican Communion as Catholic.* This is that which should call forth the love and loyalty of every member and particularly of those amongst the Clergy or considering the Sacred Ministry. Consequently Anglicans, while regarding with great respect and admiration the splendid work and real devotion of Roman Catholics, will reject Papal claims as unhistorical and unscriptural, and will rejoice that sharing with Rome this great heritage of the True Religion, it does so while avoiding all accretions to the Faith and all vain or superstitious practices contrary to Apostolic purity.

From Reformation days, perhaps before, under various names, there have been two historic parties in the Anglican Communion. They are generally referred to today as the "Protestant party" and the "Catholic party," or as "High Churchmen" and "Low Churchmen." Naturally the adherents of either group think that they most faithfully and fully represent their Communion! It may be, in justice to all, that these differing parties respectively represent different characteristics of the one body? And it is not a mere question of "externals," but rather does it concern the conception of the Church and the religious life of its members. Both groups are sources of great spiritual power and when faithful to the Doctrine, Discipline and Worship of the Church, alike contribute to the spread of the Gospel and the ministry of the

Word and the Sacraments. It might be said that the Anglo-Catholic party is distinguished by its loyalty to the authority of the Church and the Book of Common Prayer as handing down and enshrining the Faith and Practice of the Church, with its hallowed Rites and Ceremonies from the past, and that the Protestant party is conspicuous for its missionary zeal, its many sided labours and its claim to private judgments. Yet the mistake of such general designation is shown in that the Catholic group most firmly believes in missionary work and that the Protestant group loves the Church and the Prayer Book in its own way. They all believe in personal sanctification but the Catholics stress the need and help of the Sacraments in accomplishing it. Perhaps this inclusiveness of the Anglican Communion, under God, may make it win all the more souls for God. The essential things are the love of God, devotion to Our Lord, loyalty to the Church, in its Doctrine, Discipline and Worship, charity to all but above all *an ever firm refusal to compromise the Truth.*

V

SOME CHARACTERISTICS OF THE ANGLICAN COMMUNION

It has sometimes been thought that if visible union of the Christian world ever comes to pass, it will be with the Anglican Communion as the meeting place. For in its hold upon the Catholic Faith, it appeals to Catholics, and in its freedom of thought, within proper limitations it appeals to Protestants. Not that the Anglican Communion is "a middle of the road Church" but because it represents the ancient dictum of Saint Augustine: "in essentials, unity, in non-essentials diversity, in all things charity."

The most striking characteristic of the Anglican Communion is shown in the Services and in the devotional life of the people. The ideal seems to be that of dignity, beauty and simplicity in the rendering of the Services, and reverence, devotion and naturalness in the religious life of the individual. The aim is to avoid doing things in a formal, casual or mechanical way, to make the prayers and praises real and to *"worship God in Spirit and in Truth."*

The Book of Common Prayer, while far from perfect and capable of enrichment, is one of the great achievements of the Anglican Communion. A model of beautiful English, it aims to preserve the mean between too much and too little. It guards, preserves and enshrines the Ancient Faith, and *properly* read, studied and interpreted will be found explicitly to set forth in its integrity the Catholic Religion. The Services of the Church, originally in Greek or Hebrew, then made into the Latin, are now available to all "in a tongue understanded of the people." To have Services for those who speak English in their native language is an inestimable blessing and should be deeply appreciated by all. And of course, the Services should be so performed that they are clearly heard by all, as is the Church's intention.

The Mass or Holy Communion is, of course, the Service of solemn obligation because it is the Divine Institution of Christ. The Anglican Mass in some ways differs from others, but it is entitled to profound respect, for it embodies every essential thing and is most devotional.

The Daily Offices of Matins and Evensong are a simplification and remodelling of the ancient Breviary Offices, and were intended specially for the laity (although strange to say they now rarely attend them, except on Sundays). The Clergy are obligated to say these offices daily, in Church if possible.

Another characteristic of the Anglican Communion is that of individual freedom of thought, in matters *not* of the Faith. This liberty should never be allowed to degenerate into license, as would seem to be the case with some of the so-called "higher critics," whose assertions and assumptions are sometimes heretical. The rightful freedom of thought must have its limitations. It must not question matters of fact. It must bow in reverence before Divine Revelation. It must accept the Faith without quibble or qualification. It must acknowledge the Holy Catholic Church, guided by the Holy Ghost, as the supreme authority. In matters *outside* these spheres, freedom of thought may be rightly exercised. It is a blessed privilege to be able to think and to express this thought in things which are debatable or matters of opinion.

In the pursuance of this liberty, the Anglican Communion puts forth the Bible as an open book for all to read. It approves and counsels the study of the Sacred Scriptures. Written by holy men of old, guided by the Holy Ghost, the Sacred Scriptures are the inspired Word of God and are so accepted by the Church, which has stamped her imprimatur upon them. The Anglican Communion urges her members to "read, mark, learn and inwardly digest" the Scriptures, but in the spirit of faith, reverence and humility, humbly seeking the Church's guidance.

Another characteristic of the Anglican Communion is the spirit of restraint and balance shown in her recognition of the Saints, in the observance of the Church Year and the various festivals and fasts. The great festivals in honour of Our Lord are made of primary importance. The Seasons of Advent, Epiphany, Lent and Trinity are strongly emphasized. The Kalendar of Saints is simplified to include those called "Major Saints" and certain of those called "Minor Saints," which perhaps is better for the Laity than to be so inclusive, that the multiplicity of Saints' days obscures the meaning of all. One, however, of course, is free to add to the Prayer Book Kalendar, and there is a general observing of such days as Corpus Christi, the Assumption, Christ the King and All Soul's Day, which are most desirable to have included in the regular Prayer Book Kalendar.

In the ancient belief of the Invocation of Saints, the Anglican Communion distinctly teaches the true Catholic doctrine that in asking the prayers of the Saints, they can pray for us but cannot themselves grant our petitions. They must plead the Merits and ask the Mediation of Our Blessed Lord, *"Who ever liveth to make intercession for us."* This safeguards the Church from foolish superstition, and avoids alike the ignorant neglect of the Saints by Protestant bodies and the crude cults often found amongst Romanists.

This can well be illustrated by the Anglican position regarding the Blessed Virgin Mary, which follows the ancient tradition of the proper reverence due her. Those who erroneously think that they honour the Divine Son by ignoring the human Mother, have no support in the teaching and practice of the Anglican Communion. Avoiding alike all extremes, the Anglican Communion preserves the proper balance between *too much* and *too little.* It was *God* Who chose the Virgin Mary to be the instrument of the Incarnation, and gave her such unique place. It was *God* Who willed His Divine Son to assume our human nature of her substance, conceived by the Holy Ghost. It was *God* Who named Mary as *"blessed amongst women"* and as a consequence exalted the holy Mother of God to be first amongst the children of men. It was *not God* Who, as the years rolled on, either gave her undue honour, trespassing upon the prerogative of His Divine Son or neglected to give her proper reverence!

Thus in line with true tradition, the Anglican Communion safeguards this by saying that we *"worship and adore"* the Divine Son as God and Man; we *"reverence and honour"* the Human Mother as *"blessed amongst women."* Here we clearly distinguish between *The worship of praise and adoration* which can only be given to God and the *worship of honour and reverence,* which can be given to Mary, as the Mother of Our Lord, an honour and reverence that has no limits save that which can only be given to God.

The Tradition of the Blessed Virgin Mary is shown in the Prayer Book and Kalendar: in the commemoration of the Conception, the Nativity, the Annunciation, the Visitation, and the Purification, two of these Festivals having a special Collect, Epistle, Gospel and Preface. While other Festivals are not included, one's innate spirit of reverence will *add* that of the Assumption. For although unmentioned in Scripture, the faithful cannot believe that God would allow His handmaiden to suffer corruption in the grave but would take her in all her purity of soul and body into heaven.

As a consequence of this traditional honour of the Blessed Virgin in the Anglican Communion, and since omission is not prohibition, the Faithful can say the "Hail Mary" or the "Angelus," since God gave us that, and ask the prayers of Our Lady. They may say the "Rosary," although strictly speaking this is more of a devotion to Christ than to Mary, since the Holy Mysteries all relate to Him. They may have statues and before them burn votive candles to symbolize that their prayers are offered in the Name of Our Lord, the Light of the World.

Yet in all this, in all the honour and reverence that is given to her, who is sometimes called the *"Queen of Heaven"* and is referred to by the poet as *"Woman above all women glorified: our tainted nature's solitary boast,"* the Anglican Communion remembers that she is not God but the Mother of Him, Who is God. We ask her prayers and she prays for us. And since she is the dearest of all to the Sacred Heart of Jesus, her prayers avail more than those of *any* or *all* of the Saints. *Yet Our Lady herself cannot* dispense blessings or grant favours. She can only pray for us in the Name of Christ, pleading *His Merits* and asking *His Mediation,* as *"He ever liveth to make intercession for us."* He the Source and Fountain of all Grace, "our only Mediator and Advocate" as we say in the Mass.

Occasionally there are found members of the Anglican Communion, particularly amongst the Clergy, who grow restless or discontented of her balanced judgment, of her traditional position between too little and too much. Some of these become affected with that which may be called "Roman fever," and some similarly affected with "Roman phobia." The former, seeing Rome as a great historic body embracing the largest number of Christian Souls, begin to long for her system and even copy it. These become blind to historic facts, they lose hold on theological truth, they fail to realize that while Rome holds to Catholic Faith and Practice and is a tremendous power for good, yet she has added to the Creed, introduced the Silent Mass in a foreign tongue, exploits modern miracles, indulgenced prayers, superstitious practices, crude cults, and condones lower standards and commercialized ways. One may properly praise Rome for her preservation of the ancient Faith, but surely for all of the sins and shortcomings of the Anglican Communion one should not wish to exchange that body for the Papal Obedience.

Roman phobia is just as unintelligent. Those so affected refuse everything from that source. They fail to see, that without being in any way influenced by the distinctive ways of Rome, they may still adopt and practice good things therefrom. After all, Anglicans and Romanists are all members of the ancient body, the One, Holy, Catholic and Apostolic Church. Consequently anything found in either part, not contrary to the teaching of the other parts should be lawful to copy. So Anglicans do not hesitate to adopt for their own use such services as Benediction, The Three Hours Service on Good Friday, the Stations of the Cross and Tenebrae, each one specially Scriptural if studied and understood.

The Anglican Communion follows the Apostolic and Early Church in administering the Blessed Sacrament in both kinds, except when taking the Reserved Sacrament to the sick. The Book of Common Prayer definitely and distinctly teaches that the Mass is a true sacrifice offered for the living and the dead, and that after Consecration, Our Lord is Really, Supernaturally, Spiritually and Objectively Present in the Blessed Sacrament both at the Mass and when Reserved. As explained in the metaphysical term of "Concomitance," it is taught that Christ is Present, Whole and Entire, Body, Soul and Divinity in either Species of Bread or Wine. Consequently reception in one kind is a complete communion, in which Our Lord's Body and Blood are received with all the grace and blessing which appertain to the same.

In the Administration at our Anglican Mass, however, the Holy Communion is given in both kinds, according to Apostolic practice, and Our Lord's Own Institution. This, of course, is a tax in large Parishes and the Clergy may sometimes desire that it was the ordered rule to do as Rome does, administer in one kind. Yet as most of our Churches are small, the Apostolic way is easily practicable and should be followed. It is sacrilegious to suggest any danger of disease from the Chalice, for not only should we believe that Christ protects His Own Sacrament, but also Life Insurance statistics prove that the safest risks are those of the Priests, who when they celebrate Mass have to consume all that remains in the Chalice after Communion. The practice of intinction as occasionally introduced with us is to be condemned in every way, as not even being done in the manner of the Holy Orthodox Eastern Church, which has no authority with us, but as lacking reverence and refinement.

Another tradition of the Anglican Communion has always been that of a learned Clergy. One fears that this does not hold as true now as in former days, yet probably the Anglican Priesthood, generally speaking, is more highly educated and cultured than that of the other parts of the Church. The Anglican Communion never had a Thomas Aquinas or an Augustine but it did have the Venerable Bede, Alcuin and Anselm in early days; it did have Duns Scotus, great amongst the "Schoolmen'; it did have Pearson and the Caroline Divines and later such lights as Pusey, Forbes, Wordsworth, Lightfoot, Liddon, Gore, Wilberforce, Percival, Mortimer and Hall, not to mention certain great names of today.

It will be a happy day when all in the Sacred Priesthood of the Anglican Communion realize their splendid heritage and try and apply themselves to adding to the learning that has adorned the past. And in this it is hoped that they will ever have as a basis the Holy Scriptures, the writings of the Fathers, the great contributions of Theologians of all ages, sound in the Faith, and will aim to be well grounded in Latin and Greek, those dead languages which ever live in real culture, education and learning.

VI

THE MINISTRY

It is most important to understand the nature of the Priesthood, as related to the Church, the mystical body of Christ. As the Church is not a man-made organization but the divine institution of our Blessed Lord, so the Priest is not a mere minister but rather the representative and ambassador of Jesus Christ, Our Blessed Lord acting through him in all of his ministerial functions. The Priest, ordained through the laying on of hands of the Bishop, continuing the Apostolic Succession, stands forth vested in the Authority of the Church.

Since the Anglican Communion is part of the One, Holy, Catholic and Apostolic Church and holds the True Religion, her Clergy are "Catholic Priests," not "Protestant Ministers." It is unfortunate that so many people do not know that the only authoritative use of the word "Protestant," in the Episcopal Church, is in the subtitle to "The Book of Common Prayer and Administration of the Sacraments and Other Rites and Ceremonies of the Church," as a protest to the unwarranted claims of Rome and the errors of other bodies. The word "Protestant" is not used in the Services or found in the context of the Prayer Book.

Thus, in the Office called "The Form and Manner of Ordering Priests," one is to be ordained as a Priest, admitted to "The Order of Priesthood," and the Church is referred to as the mystical body of Christ as "His Church," "This Church," or "Thy Church." And the authoritative and sacramental character of the Office is shown by the actual words of Ordination, the Bishop saying: *"Receive the Holy Ghost for the Office and Work of a Priest in the Church of God, now committed unto thee by the Imposition of our hands. Whose sins thou dost forgive, they are forgiven and whose sins thou dost retain, they are retained. And be thou a faithful Dispenser of the Word of God and of His Holy Sacraments, in the Name of the Father and of the Son and of the Holy Ghost. Amen.".*

The Preface to the Ordinal well sums up the teaching of the Church, which has very properly safeguarded entrance into the Sacred Ministry that so far as possible unworthy or unsuitable men may not be admitted to the Priesthood: "It is evident unto all men diligently reading Holy Scripture and ancient Authors that from the Apostles' time there have been these Orders of Ministers in Christ's Church—Bishops, Priests and Deacons. Which Offices were evermore had in such reverend estimation that no man might presume to execute any of them, except he were first called, tried, examined and known to have such qualities as are requisite for the same; an dalso by public Prayer, with Imposition of Hands, were approved and admitted thereunto by lawful Authority. And therefore, to the intent that these Orders may be continued and reverently used and esteemed in this Church, no man shall be accounted or taken to be a lawful Bishop, Priest or Deacon in this Church or suffered to execute any of the said Functions except he be called, tried, examined and admitted thereunto according to the Form hereafter following or hath had Episcopal Consecration or Ordination."

Such a declaration as this clearly shows the *intention* of the Anglican Communion to hold and minister the Sacrament of Holy Orders according to the teaching and practice of the Holy Catholic Church, of which it is a part. It also plainly debars any and all of the wrong proposals put forth for the cause of unity which would lower, change or alter these ancient and necessary requirements.

In the Service called "The Form and Manner of Ordering Priests," there is put into practice the declarations of the Preface. Those long time in the Ministry may well often read over this Service to their spiritual profit.

Here is given the Commission of the Holy Catholic Church to those called to the Sacred Ministry, who in the previous part of the Ordination Service were charged to be "Messengers, Watchmen and Stewards of the Lord; to teach and to premonish, to feed and to provide for the Lord's family; to seek for Christ's sheep that are dispersed abroad and for His children, who are in the midst of this naughty world," to "have always therefore in your remembrance how great a treasure is committed to your charge," "that ye never cease your labour, your care and diligence," "to sanctify the lives of you and yours and to fashion them after the Rule and Doctrine of Christ, that ye may be wholesome and godly examples and patterns for the people to follow," and they must remember to watch for those in their charge "as for those they must give account."

Thus, those in Holy Orders and those who are thinking of "the call" should realize the continuity of the Holy Catholic Church, and thrill with the knowledge that the Clergy today are one with those who have served the Lord in the Sacred Ministry through almost two thousand years, in the following and the companionship of many great and glorious Saints. Far different is this from the ministry of those bodies which have come with the Reformation or subsequently, which for all their good works, is not one with the Ministry of the Ancient and Apostolic Church, the Divine Institution of Christ, as seen in the Anglican, Eastern and Roman Communions.

As a Priest of the Catholic Church, therefore, and not as a Minister of a Protestant body, he who is called to the Sacred Ministry goes forth as the accredited agent of Our Blessed Lord, to speak in His Name and to act through His power. Surely the picture must be inspiring to one who wishes in such capacity to serve the Lord Christ and do one's best for the Glory of God and the love of Souls.

Contrary to that which some people think, the Church's Services occupy the smallest portion of a Priest's time, although, of course, the most important part of his life. There is the Daily Mass, there is the recital of the Daily Office and there is the time given to private devotions, meditation and intercessions. Then there are the hours devoted to study, reading and the preparation of Sermons. This forms the general rule of life that should seldom vary, yet through the constant round of festival and fast in the Church it never grows monotonous but rather year by year more beautiful, attractive and inspiring. It should be a joy and blessing to stand day by day at the Altar to offer up the Holy Sacrifice for the living and the dead and to receive Our Lord in the Holy Communion, a duty and a precious privilege which should bring forth fruit in a more consecrated life of Service.

Then comes that which may be called the variable duty, for no day knows what another day will bring forth. Now it is a baptism or a marriage. Or it may be a funeral with the singing of a Solemn Requiem. Or some sudden call to see a sick or dying person. Or a rush to a hospital, or a visit to a prison. Then again it may be the preparation of a Confirmation Class, the attending of Guild meetings, the hearing of Confessions or calling upon one's parishioners. A Priest's duties, like those of a Doctor, can never be fully set forth, and a Priest's contacts, even more than those of a Doctor, are variable, interesting and illuminating. No one more than a Priest comes to a better understanding of the many kinds of character and the many vagaries of human nature. He sees the worst as well as the best. He should be easily accessible at any time to those who wish to see him and he should cultivate the patience, tact and sympathy so necessary.

In the Service of Ordination, while the form in the Ordinal is always followed, the outward observance in the matter of ceremonial often varies. Sometimes everything is very simply done. At other times there is a revival of ancient ritual, such as the Ordinand being clothed in the Chasuble and handed a Chalice and Paten, this last being called "the Tradition of the Instruments," and other things. Yet whether with little or much ceremonial, the one ordained becomes a Priest of the Holy Catholic Church, and is vested in her authority to minister the Word and the Sacraments and have the cure of Souls. Consequently one should ever remember that while the most noble thing a man can be is to be a good Priest, helpful alike to the Church and the world, there is nothing worse, more harmful and inimical to God or that does more injury to souls than a bad Priest!

VII

THE SCRIPTURES AND CREED

THE ANGLICAN COMMUNION lays great stress upon the Sacred Scriptures, in the Devotional Services of the Church and in the Ordination of Priests.

The Bible is the Inspired Word of God, written by holy men of old, guided by the Holy Ghost. Its various parts were gathered together and put forth by the Holy Catholic Church *"the pillar and ground of truth"* as the Divine Revelation of God. It comes therefore upon the Authority of the Church, which has stamped its imprimatur upon it.

It is like no other book. It is the creation of centuries. The Old Testament in Hebrew and the New Testament in Greek reveal and combine two great cultures. The contents embrace history, prophecy, poetry, praise and the record of Our Lord's Life, Works and Words. There is a beauty, a simplicity, a majesty, a depth that make the Bible unique and that carries a conviction of its truth. No other written works have been so read and studied as have been the Scriptures and no others have so stood the test of time. This can lead to only one conclusion: that the Bible is what the Church claims it to be: the Inspired and Infallible Word of God, the Divine Revelation received and recorded by human agents, guided by the Holy Ghost.

No writings have ever been so carefully guarded and treasured. The Jews most zealously watched over the rolls of the Old Testament. The Christians likewise prized the manuscripts of the New Testament. As a consequence the Church has inherited the traditional Scriptures, handed down from age to age, from century to century, so safeguarded that one has every reason to accept them as authentic.

The Old Testament, originally written in Hebrew but later translated into Greek (in the famous Septuagint Version), was supplemented by the New Testament written in Greek. The original copies of all of these writings have long since been lost but their content of both words and teaching has been preserved in many valuable copies, versions and corroborative records.

First, there are three very ancient Greek Uncial Manuscripts, probably dating back to the fourth or fifth centuries, called respectively: the *"Alexandrian,"* the *"Vatican"* and the *"Sinaitic"* and belonging in the order named to the Anglican, the Roman and the Eastern Communions.

Then there are many Ancient Versions, the most important of these probably being the Latin "Vulgate," the work of Saint Jerome in the fourth century. And supplementing these are the innumerable lengthy quotations to be found in the Writings of the Ancient Fathers and the great Doctors and Theologians.

There were certain very early translations of the Scriptures into English, notably that of the Venerable Bede in the eighth century and that of Wycliffe in the fourteenth century but the English language has changed so much that these could only be read with difficulty by the average person.

The Reformation saw many translations into English, such as those of Tyndale, Coverdale and the Great Bible. Subsequent revisions have been made in later times. For rhythmic beauty no translation has ever equalled that known as the King James Version, of the Seventeenth Century.

Before the invention of Printing by Gutenberg in the fifteenth century all of the copies of the Bible were made by hand, chiefly by Scribes in the Monasteries and Convents, who often did the most beautifully illuminated work and by their intense religious devotion made their labours a work of love. As a consequence they took the greatest pains to ensure accuracy. Nevertheless occasional mistakes were made, errors in copying occurred, wrong readings escaped notice, although eventually corrected by a comparison of the many existing versions and translations. And one may well believe that God, Who gave us the Scriptures, has Providentially preserved them intact for the use and edification of the Faithful, even as He guided the compilers of the Bible by the Holy Ghost so as to know which were the Inspired Writings, the real Revelation of God.

In reading and interpreting the Sacred Scriptures, the Church, not the individual, must be the guide. For different parts must be taken in different ways: some portions in a literal sense, some in a spiritual sense, some in a metaphorical sense, always remembring that *"no scripture is of private interpretation."* And the Priest as well as the layman must remember his human limitation when reading, especially in what may be called "the hard places." For instance, when one comes upon many things in the Old Testament which seem strange or at variance with our conception of God and His relations with man, we should realize that God is dealing with primitive peoples, whose understanding was faulty; that our western minds think in different terms from those in the east "for never the twain shall meet," that often imagery or figures of speech are used and must be so taken; and that the Old Testament was but the preparation for the New (the full revelation of the partial earlier one), even as Our Lord said He came *"to fulfil the Law and the Prophets."*

Because some Scriptures are very difficult to modern readers is no reason why they should be impugned, for surely when one thinks the matter out and realizes that the Bible is a progressive revelation covering thousands of years he must be content to *"see but in a glass darkly."*

In the reading and study of the Scriptures, it must always be remembered that the Church gave us the Bible, not the Bible the Church. Consequently the Scriptures cannot be quoted against the Church but must be interpreted in agreement with the Church's teaching. And so assured is the Church's position that the Church instructs her Clergy *"to teach nothing as necessary to eternal salvation but that which can be concluded and proved by the Scriptures"* and *"to banish and drive away all strange doctrines contrary to God's word."* Thus the Creeds, the Liturgies, the Traditions, the Scriptures all work together and set forth the True Religion or that which is called the Catholic Faith. Since the Church is a Divine Institution, the Mystical Body of Christ, the Pillar and Ground of Truth, the Preserver of Faith, the Dispenser of Grace, the Guide in Morals, her imprimatur upon the Sacred Scriptures, her authoritative approval of them, make their acceptance binding as "*de fide*" upon all Christian people, and makes the Church the interpreter of them.

The Clergy must be prepared to defend the Bible from attacks both from within and without the Church, from those who do not understand the Scriptures, from those who dislike the teachings as reflecting upon their own lives and opinions, and also from the so-called higher critics and scholars, some of whom, carried away by their academic theories, assume and assert doubts as to the authenticity and accuracy of the Bible, discredit revelation, deny the supernatural and often unconsciously play with heresy. The Clergy should be able to answer all objections, to show the impossibility of proving the adverse assertions and to stress the fact that the *acceptance throughout the centuries is a strong presumption of the truth of the Scriptures*.

If any of the higher critics see this book and have a sense of humour they may enjoy this: a poorly educated woman said to the writer, "I see they are giving a big dinner to Heretics in New York!" "What in the world do you mean?" The woman pointed to a newspaper which had a heading: "Big dinner to Higher Critics."

In recent years strong corroborative evidence has come from Archaeology. Through excavations in the Far East, the Cuneiform Tablets unearthed have repeatedly proved the accuracy of the Scriptural stories. The Tablets and hieroglyphic records have

shown an oriental culture and literature of a very
early date, anteceding that of Greece and Rome.
Here one finds that the Israelites had considerable
contact with the Egyptians, Babylonians and As-
syrians, and that these have similar accounts of certain events such as the creation and the deluge.

It has been assumed by some that the advance
in scientific discovery has discredited certain of the
contents of the Bible, such as the Old Testament
stories. This is quite a mistake. Science and Scripture are complementary, not contradictory, the first
largely theory, the latter revelation. Human science
is *relative truth* to finite minds. Religion is *absolute
truth* in the Infinite Mind of God. Given God, as
the Creator and Maker of all things, He who ordained the Laws which govern the universe can
suspend those Laws at His will. That which is supernatural to man is natural with God. Thus the Old
Testament stories become easy of credence, quite as
one would expect in a primitive prehistoric age.
And these are tied up with the New Testament and
the Services of the Church. For instance, the beautiful and picturesque story of Adam and Eve, in the
two creations (the *body "from the dust of the
ground,"* and the *soul,* the *breathing in "of the
breath of life"*), not only teaches "the Fall of man
from original righteousness," but predicts the Incarnation and the Redemption in that *"the Seed of the
woman should bruise the serpent's head."* Adam
and Eve are written into the Baptismal Office, based
upon a belief in "the Fall," and in the Burial Office,
in the beautiful lesson from the Corinthians. So
with the Story of Noah and the Ark, referred to by
Saint Peter, and of Jonah in the whale's belly, re-

ferred to by Our Lord. Surely *"with God all things are possible."* Given that belief every part of the Bible is easy of acceptance.

Our Blessed Lord endorsed the Old Testament Scriptures and constantly referred to them and quoted them. He said *"Search the Scriptures for they are they which testify of Me."* And once, in referring to the Pentateuch, He said: *"Had ye believed Moses, ye would have believed Me, for he wrote of Me; But if ye believe not his writings how shall ye believe My words."* Here our Lord seems to anticipate attacks! And Canon Liddon, in condemning their assertion and assumption, once wrote: "How is such a supposition reconciled with the authority of Him, who has so solemnly commended to us the Books of Moses and whom Christians believe to be *too wise to be Himself deceived* and *too good to deceive His creatures.*" It has well been said: "Unbelievers have always begun by slighting the Old Testament. Let any tempted to do so, remember that the Old and New must stand or fall together; and that those who attack the Old Testament are knocking away the foundations of Christianity itself."

The acceptance of the Scriptures is necessary to our belief in Our Lord. He came as the Saviour and He knew that He was the Messiah. He said that He was to fulfil the Law and the Prophets. He showed that He was God as well as Man, when He calmed the winds and the waves, when He raised the dead, when He absolved from sin, and when He said to the Samaritan Woman, *"I am the Resurrection and the Life."* Blasphemous, rash and sacrilegious then are those who think Our Lord's knowledge limited. The Church teaches that Our Lord (One Person with Two Natures) had "Beatific Knowledge" as God, "Acquired Knowledge" as Man, and in addition "Infused Knowledge" but *always He who spoke was the Second Person of the Trinity, God, Who knew all things.* Everyone should remember this!

It is an old saying that we pray as we believe. The devotional life of the Church testifies to the truth of the Scriptures. The services are based upon a belief in the Bible. This is seen in the use of the Scriptures in the Epistles, the Gospels, the Lessons and the Prayers. For centuries, and especially since the discovery of printing, have countless thousands found cheer, comfort and courage in the Word of God and in its use in the Services of the Church. The beauty, the simplicity, the majesty of the Bible convince of its truth. The very Miracles are but the supernatural revelation of our Lord's Divinity, mostly great acts of healing showing His love.

And why after hundreds of years should attacks be made today upon the long accepted Word of God? For surely those who "compiled" and put forth the Scriptures had a better access to the ancient writings and a better understanding of them and their origins than those of the present day! It has long been an axiom that the nearer the source, the greater the accuracy and comprehension. And surely no reverently minded person can believe that God would have allowed the Church and the Faithful to have laboured under a delusion for centuries! How can one think that God has hidden the real knowledge of the Scriptures until our own times! Those who put them forth were as surely guided by God the Holy Ghost as were those who wrote them! And the great Fathers, Schoolmen and Theologians of all time, who so often quoted and referred to the Scriptures would surely not have done so if any doubt could have been cast upon their accuracy or authenticity.

Given God *"with whom all things are possible,"* the difficulties disappear, whether they be stories, miracles or teachings beyond our understanding, for He is from above, we from below, He is infinite, we finite, and we must submit our mind to the Mind of God. For the very reason that the Sacred Scriptures contain many things above and beyond man's understanding is why they should be humbly accepted as a Divine Revelation, the Inspired and Infallible Word of God. The faithful will "read, mark, learn and inwardly digest the Scriptures, that by patience and comfort of God's Holy Word they may ever hold fast the blessed hope of everlasting life," and those in the Ministry, as they study and meditate upon them, will ever do so humbly and reverently, saying: *"Lord I believe: help Thou my unbelief."* *"Thou art the Way, the Truth, and the Life."* God will speak to them through His Holy Word. Our Lord will reveal Himself to them. Perhaps they will feel as did the two Disciples who were joined by Our Lord on the road to Emmaus, after His Resurrection: *"Did not our heart burn within us while He talked with us by the way and while He opened to us the Scriptures."*

The Bible figures largely in the life of a Priest. He must be a student of it. He must be an expounder of it. And he must remember that only by approaching with a meek, lowly and humble heart, with faith, love and devotion, will he ever gain the inspiration and illumination that therein is found. *"Search the Scriptures for in them ye think ye have eternal life: and they are they which testify of Me."* They make men *"wise unto salvation,"* and are a great reservoir of truth, containing *"all Doctrine required as necessary for eternal Salvation through faith in Jesus Christ"* and that *"may be concluded and proved by the same."* It is in the diligent study of the Scriptures, that next to the Sacramental life keeps the soul in closest union with God.

THE WORD OF GOD is also set forth in the Creed, which in its original form preceded the New Testament. By the Creed is meant the short summary of the main doctrine of the Church as set forth in the three forms called respectively the Apostles' Creed, the Nicene Creed and the Athanasian Creed. The Apostles' Creed was the simple declaration of the Early Church and is that used in most of the devotional offices today. The Nicene Creed (the greater part put forth by the Council of Nice in 325 and the latter part by the Council of Constantinople in 381), is that which more explicitly sets forth the belief of the Church, particularly as regards the Divinity of Our Lord, Jesus Christ. The Athanasian Creed, expressing the teaching of Saint Athanasius (the Defender of the Faith at the Council of Nice), was probably written by Saint Hilary of Poictiers, and is a still more full exposition of the Faith.

The Creed is not a matter of individual choice. It is in content, the Divine Revelation of Our Blessed Lord. In form it rests upon the Authority of the Holy Catholic Church. It is a belief because in great part it could not be known through human knowledge but is of God and teaches of God and the Nature, Attributes and the Things of God. Its statements are Holy Mysteries because they are beyond our understanding. Yet each and every article of the Creed is to be accepted as the Church has declared it. The denial or rejection of any one part puts the soul in peril, for it is *"the Faith once for all delivered to the Saints"* by Our Lord.

The Creed is no mere symbol. Belief expresses itself in conduct. There is no greater mistake than to minimize the influence of one's belief. The Creed affects not only the understanding but also the character and the life. Consequently the Church expects those in the Sacred Ministry not only themselves to hold fast the Faith in its integrity, but also continually to teach and preach this Faith to those committed to their charge. It is essential to both Clergy and Laity to know what is the belief of the Church, and to accept this in full conviction of its truth, as *"the Faith of the Gospel."*

To illustrate: how vague sometimes is the presentation of the four great doctrines concerning Our Lord: the Incarnation, the Redemption, the Resurrection and the Ascension, and especially, for instance, as to the "Virgin Birth," and the Bodily Resurrection of Christ, both of which are explicit and implicit in the Creed and should be firmly maintained. Saint Augustine referred to Blessed Mary as *"a Virgin Conceiving, a Virgin bringing forth and a Virgin dying."* The Virgin Birth was necessary to the integrity of the Incarnation, to cut off the entail of original sin. This is a doctrine "*de fide.*" And also, while perhaps not more than a pious opinion, is the belief, which appeals to every reverently minded person, that the Blessed Virgin was supernaturally sanctified at the very moment of Conception, to give a spotless substance to her Divine Son. Of course, no informed person should confound "the Virgin Birth" of Our Lord with the "Immaculate Conception" of the Blessed Virgin.

In the Resurrection, there is often a confusion of thought, due to not understanding the conditions of Our Lord's Risen Body, notwithstanding that they are plainly stated in the Scriptural Account. Thus Christ rose in the identical body, that had been born of the Virgin Mary and had hung upon the Cross but then with the new properties theologically defined as: "*Impassibility*" (He could no longer suffer), "*Subtlety*" (He could pass through solid substances as the rock of the Sepulchre and the barred doors), "*Agility*" (He could be anywhere at will), "*Glory*" (He was full of beauty and majesty).

Those who find their faith weak before that which passes human understanding, should remember that the great doctrines of the Creed are "*Holy Mysteries*," that "*with God all things are possible*," that "*God's ways are wonderful and past finding out.*" Happy is he, who at the close of a long and devoted ministry, can say with Saint Paul: "*I have kept the Faith*," to realize the prophetic words of Saint Augustine: "*Here believe: there understand!*"

VIII

THE SACRAMENTS

THE SACRAMENTS are no mere forms. They are Holy Mysteries, really beyond our understanding, under outward and visible forms conveying inward and spiritual grace, each one specially fulfilling the purpose for which ordained. Thus they are vital powers, extending Our Lord's work in the world in a sacramental way. Consequently the Seven Sacraments of Holy Baptism, Holy Absolution or Penance, Holy Confirmation, Holy Communion, Holy Matrimony, Holy Orders and Holy Unction are realities in the spiritual life, the very expression of the true religion.

Those already in the Ministry and those considering this Sacred Calling should have a clear and proper understanding of the Sacraments, of the "form, matter and intention," necessary to each one and of that which the several Sacraments are expected to do and effect. And they must also realize that, as with a devout layman so even more so with a devout priest, the Sacramental Life must be regarded as the main one through which the spiritual being can grow and flourish and bring forth the fruits and graces of the Christian Religion which we call *the beauty of holiness.* Confession, Communion and the Sacrifice of the Altar are therefore

51

essential to the life and character and work of the faithful Priest.

In a book of this kind, it is not necessary to set forth the meaning of the Sacraments or that which they accomplish, which all of the Clergy and those thinking of the Sacred Ministry are supposed to know. It may be helpful, however, to accentuate the following as showing how the Sacraments are vital powers for conferring Divine Grace: *Holy Baptism*, regeneration or rebirth in Christ, taking away original sin and making the recipient "a member of Christ, the child of God and an inheritor of the Kingdom of Heaven"; *Holy Absolution* or Penance, Christ's forgiveness of sins conveyed through His Priest as His representative or ambassador who speaks in His stead to those coming in true Faith, Love and Repentance; *Holy Confirmation*, the Sevenfold Gift of the Holy Ghost, to those who renew the solemn promise and vow made in their name at Baptism; *Holy Communion*, the Sacrament of the Body and Blood of Christ really, supernaturally and objectively Present under the forms of Bread and Wine, and the Sacrifice of the Altar commemorating Our Lord's Death and Passion of the Cross; *Holy Order*, the Special Gift and Commission of the Holy Ghost for the Office and Work of a Deacon, or a Priest or a Bishop; *Holy Matrimony*, the blessing and sanctifying power of God faithfully to fulfil the purposes of marriage; *Holy Unction*, the anointing with Oil blessed by a Bishop for the help and strengthening of the body and soul of the recipient. The knowledge of what the Sacraments really are and do is a very great help to the proper regard for the same and the recognition of the supernatural aids in the Church.

The holy Sacrifice of the Altar is of course the greatest Sacrament of all. It has been variously called "the Holy Communion," "the Holy Eucharist," "the Holy Mysteries," "the Blessed Sacrament" and "the Mass," these names generally denoting certain aspects of this, Our Lord's Own Service. At the English Reformation, in the First Prayer Book of Edward VI, in 1549, the title was *"The Supper of the Lord, and the Holy Communion, commonly called the Mass."* This last name, being short, descriptive and by tradition embodying most of the other meanings, has very much to commend it and in the Anglican Church is coming more and more into general use. No intelligent person can rightfully object to its use, or will fail to see how expressive and adaptable it is.

A great many people, even some of the Clergy, have to learn what the Mass or Holy Communion really is! Too often they look upon it as just a "Service," in which the Sacramental belief is fulfilled in partaking of the outward elements accompanied with a prayerful communing with God! When one thinks of Our Lord's teaching as recorded in the sixth chapter of the Gospel of Saint John and of the accounts of the Institution in the Upper Room and of Saint Paul's reference to the Sacrament, such faith and practice is really a perfect parody!

For according to Christ's Own Institution, the Mass or Holy Communion is both a Sacrifice and a Sacrament, not a mere Service but a Holy Mystery in which Our Lord works and acts through His Priest at the Altar. As has already been said as a Sacrifice it is the memorial of Christ's Passion and

Death on the Cross, mystically identical with it, and as a Sacrament it is the Communion of the Body and Blood of Our Lord, Really and Objectively but Supernaturally Present under the forms of Bread and Wine. The record of Scripture will not bear any other interpretation than this.

Consequently both Priests and People should reverence the Holy Mass. They should seek to be present at the Offering. They should longingly receive the Gift. Mass and Communion should be the very centre of their religious life, as they hear Our Lord from His Altar Throne saying: *"Lo: I am with you alway."* Every Priest should realize the great blessing of the daily Mass and Communion, according to the Apostolic use. The spiritual gain in so doing is beyond words. There will come a supernatural strength and a divine illumination that will chasten and beautify one's religion. And many a problem has been solved, and the way shown as the Priest stands before the Altar celebrating Mass or in the Choir saying the Offices. For God speaks to the Soul in worship. Not to *wish* to offer the Holy Communion or to read the Divine Office is one of the most serious reflections that could be cast upon any Priest! It would seem to reflect upon his ministerial vocation, which is based upon a life of prayer.

This stressing of the Mass is to show that while all of the Sacraments are great means of grace, the Holy Communion stands out preeminently. *"It is the Mass that matters."*

This should have as its underlying motive the perfecting of his spiritual union with Our Blessed Lord, the living a *"life hid with Christ in God."*

The belief and worship of the Church centers in Our Blessed Lord Jesus Christ, Who is Perfect God and Perfect Man. Like a magnet, He is to attract souls to Himself and in Himself bring them to God. Everyone consequently must come to know, follow and love Our Lord and have a real personal relationship with Him. He must not be thought of only as the Son of God or the Son of Mary, or as the Founder of the Church, or even as the Saviour of the world, He must be seen as *our* Lord, *our* Saviour, *our* Master, *our* Friend, *our* Brother, and we must be united with Him and live and dwell in Him through the holiest bonds of love, devotion, thanksgiving and adoration. He must be the daily companion. Without any pose, cant or hypocrisy, a Priest must in a very real sense be walking with Him day by day, so that Our Lord is at once the Guide, the Strengthener, the Sanctifier and the ultimate goal of his life. This should be the blessed privilege of *every* Soul. This especially should be the experience of *every* Priest. He feels Christ within him. He sees Christ about him in everyone to whom he ministers. He prays and works and worships in the close companionship of Him, Who, through that prayer, work and worship, is preparing him for everlasting life, the joy of enjoying Him in His revealed splendor forever in Heaven. He must ever remember that a Priest cannot make others know, love or follow the Master unless he himself first knows, loves and follows Him. One cannot give to others things one himself has not received. All of which reflection accentuates the need of the Holy Mass and the Divine Office, as a reminder and an inspiration to every Priest.

A Parish, in which there are daily Masses and on Sundays both Low Mass and High Mass, will show a sacramental life very different from that of the type of Parish in which this seems to be of secondary consideration. Where the Clergy are day by day offering at the Altar this great Sacrifice for the living and the dead, the people will begin to come, and little by little there will be formed groups who never miss a daily Mass. Consequently, the Clergy should realize their responsibility in this respect, for their own devotion leads to the devotion of the people and their failure to have their daily Mass prevents the people from developing their own Sacramental life.

The late Mass on Sundays should be regarded by the Priest who takes it as a great privilege. It may mean a somewhat long fast but those Priests who regularly sing this Service rarely think of this or feel in any way inconvenienced. This late Mass may be a Solemn High Mass with the traditional "Three Sacred Ministers: Celebrant, Deacon and Sub-Deacon," or a Sung Mass with incense, with one Priest, the Celebrant, officiating. This generally depends upon the size of the Parish and the number of Clergy available. To many of the Congregation, there is no preference, as there is little difference in the Service. Yet there are some who think that the Sung Mass is more devotional and less distracting. Either one helps to dignify and exalt Sunday by the "Lord's Own Service" on the "Lord's Own Day."

IX

THE WORSHIP OF GOD

THE WORSHIP OF GOD, called Divine Worship, is for the Glory of God, the Honour of Christ, the acknowledgment of God's Sovereignty and the offering of prayer and sacrifice for the Living and the Dead.

God in a measure has revealed how He wishes to be worshipped. From Mt. Sinai He gave unto Moses His directions which were expressed in the Rites and Ceremonies of the Jewish Dispensation. As set forth they were but the types and shadows of the fuller revelation which came in the Christian Church. Our Lord attended the Worship of the Temple. He said that He came to "fulfil the Law and the Prophets." This He did by His Life and Teaching, in which the Jewish Sacrifices were replaced by Our Lord's Death and Passion on the Cross and the Holy Communion or Mass that is the perpetual Memorial of it, and by His Counsels and Commands given to His followers as the content of the Christian Religion, the Catholic Faith. So that the revelation given in principle to Moses found its full and complete expression in Our Lord and His Teaching.

The Apostolic Church, as recorded in the Acts, had a Daily Communion Service and daily Prayers. Thus from the very beginning, Our Lord's Own

Service, the only one of Divine Institution, was celebrated daily. So one may say: *"It is the Mass that matters."* The Daily Prayers came to be the Apostolic Hours, three times a day, at Morning, Noon and Night. To these in early times there were added various Litanies.

In the Early and Middle Ages, through the rise of the Monastic Orders, these Offices were expanded into those of the Breviary, following the words of the Psalmist, *"Seven times a day will I praise Thee."* These "Seven Canonical Offices" were known as Matins (Lauds), Prime, Tierce, Sexts, Nones, Vespers and Compline. These with the Mass were the Services in the Western Church at the Reformation, but while all of them were said by the Clergy, whether Secular or Religious, the only Service generally had by the people was the Apostolic and historic one of the Mass as of solemn obligation because of Divine Institution.

Here then is seen the Worship of God as set forth and practiced by the Holy Catholic Church from age to age. Not by individual whim or preference but by order and authority. So that the Rites and Ceremonies that enshrine the Worship of God are hallowed and sanctified by the use of centuries, making for a continuity throughout the ages.

In Reformation times, the Church of England did not break with the Church, but reformed herself within that body. Consequently in revising the Services of the Church, and translating them into English, no radical departure was made from ancient usage. The Holy Communion, *"commonly called the Mass,"* was still set forth as the chief Service of the Church, and called *"our bounden duty."* And the

Seven Canonical Offices of the Breviary, that had been an expansion of the three Apostolic Hours of ancient times, were now condensed, simplified and put forth as two, Matins and Evensong, with the Litany to be used on certain days.

Sometimes, when one surveys the different Services in different Parishes, one wonders why such large variation and why in some places so many opportunities are given for Worship and in others so few. And the question is sometimes asked: Is there no law or authority in the matter? The answer is most clear and explicit. The Book of Common Prayer has distinctly and definitely set forth that which is regularly expected, speaking with no uncertain voice.

To know the Prayer Book is to know the rule of the Anglican Communion. There is the Order for *Daily Morning Prayer*, and *Daily Evening Prayer*, often referred to as Matins and Evensong, *the Litany* to be used on Sundays, Wednesdays and Fridays and the *Holy Communion or the Mass*, with Collects, Epistles and Gospels for Sundays, Holy Days and Saints' Days. Since it was the Apostolic custom as related in the Acts to have a daily Communion, and since this has always been the general practice in the Church, it is confidently to be assumed that the intention of the Prayer Book is for a daily Mass. This should not be a matter of Churchmanship. It should have nothing to do with varying views. *It should simply be regarded by all as the regular rule, in accord with the example of the Apostles.* To have this the general practice is to stress the continuity of the Church, and of the Anglican Communion as holding the True Religion.

It can hardly be questioned that the Clergy should desire and try to do as the Prayer Book directs. Every Parish should provide for these privileges of Prayer and Sacrament. The constant round of festival and fast will prevent the observance from growing monotonous. Daily will the Church's scheme of Worship prove more beautiful, edifying and inspiring. The Clergy will find it their greatest joy to stand before the Altar day by day to offer up the Holy Sacrifice for the Living and the Dead and to receive Our Lord in the Holy Communion of His Body and Blood. And the people who attend the daily Mass or the daily Offices will, like the Priest, soon find themselves increasing in that *"beauty of holiness, without which, no one can see God."*

It is inexcusable to have a closed Church, open only on Sundays and Special Days. The Church should *always be open* (except of course at night), both for the stated daily Services and also for private devotion. And it should be realized what a joy and privilege it is to the faithful and the religiously inclined to have perpetual Reservation in a Parish, where one can often find that *"peace past understanding,"* in the Presence of the Blessed Sacrament.

The rendering of the Services is an important adjunct to worship, whether the Office or Mass is said or sung. The Scriptures say that everything should be *"done decently and in order."*

This applies to the appointments of the Altar and Church, the Vestments of the Clergy and others, the details of Ritual and Ceremonial. The Clergy should understand the "Technique" of Worship. They should realize that these things are good manners in the House of God. There is no excuse for a "Sloppy

Service," or worshipping God "in any old way." It is not a matter of individual preference. Laziness, ignorance or prejudice cannot be pardoned. It is the *duty of all to know, understand and follow the Church's ordered way* (which is so full of dignity, beauty and reverence), hallowed by the use of centuries. In a home one approves of flowers, candles, music and attractive dressing, and especially on an outstanding occasion. How much more should one endorse flowers, candles, music, vestments, incense and all the accessories of worship in the House of God. And especially when we adore Our Lord in the Holy Sacrifice and Sacrament of the Altar! The failure to give God of our best as His due, must be repugnant to Him, Who in His Revelation has pictured to us the glorious worship of Heaven.

It is very unfortunate that some regard these things as a matter of Churchmanship! It should not be so. A properly appointed Altar, a properly vested Priest, the reverent use of ritual and ceremonial should be the heritage and privilege of all. And the Clergy should teach and practice this hallowed use which the Church hands down from age to age. *"This is the House of God," "The Lord is in His Holy Temple."* There should be the proper approach to God, the giving Him the honour which is His due, as the Sovereign King of Kings and Lord of Lords.

That which has been said, applies primarily to the Holy Communion Service or the Mass. The Choir Offices of Matins and Evensong are much simpler, especially when said "plain" or "read." When sung or "intoned" they become very lovely and fulfil the words of the "Venite": *"O come let us sing unto the Lord."* Solemn Evensong can be made very impressive.

Worship in its highest sense must be that of Sacrifice. According to the ancient and Scriptural requirements, there must be an Altar, there must be a Priest, there must be a Victim, there must be the shedding of blood. All of this was fulfilled in the Jewish Sacrifices offered to God. All of this was fulfilled in the real Sacrifice which replaced them, Our Lord's Death and Passion on Calvary, where He was Priest and Victim, the Altar was the Cross and His Own Precious Blood shed forth. All of this is mystically fulfilled in the Sacrifice of the Mass or Holy Communion, where, as Saint Paul says, *"We do show forth the Lord's Death,"* where Christ, ministering through the Priest at the Altar, offers the Perpetual Memorial of His Death and Passion, the *"full, perfect and sufficient Sacrifice, oblation and satisfaction for the sins of the whole world."* Consequently all right-thinking people will realize the obligation, the privilege and the blessing of the Mass or Communion Service and will wish to see it celebrated day by day, in fulfillment of Our Lord's Command: *"Do this in remembrance of me."*

For a Priest to say the Mass daily will be an inspiration to all. Not only will he himself be richly blessed, as daily at the Altar he receives Him, Whom he some day hopes to possess, enjoy and worship forever in His revealed splendour in Heaven, but he will by his example attract more and more of his Congregation themselves to attend upon the Altar. And it should be realized by all of the Clergy that one of the best tests of the spiritual and religious life in his Parish is the devotion of the people to the daily Mass, their continual coming to worship and receive their Divine Lord in these Holy Mysteries.

The ceremonial associated with the Mass is largely traditional and has been hallowed by the use of centuries. This should be studied and understood by the Clergy and the Candidates for Holy Orders and reverently practiced as a fitting accompaniment of this Sacred Service. These ceremonies are not empty forms. They are the symbolic expression of devotion. Our Lord's presence at the Temple Worship is an approval as it were, by anticipation of the beautiful ceremonial of the Holy Catholic Church. For the complete worship of God, body and soul must each have its part. So Architecture and Music came to be consecrated to the Church. So Rites and Ceremonies came into being, beautiful and stately forms accompanied with Lights, Incense, Vestments, Flowers and other adjuncts that make Worship inspiring and impressive.

Another thing to be realized and remembered by the Clergy is that religion is not static but develops with the ages. The content of the revelation is unchangeable but its expression is capable of enlargement. Consequently, there come other privileges and blessings as the need requires, which the Parish Priest should welcome, should see extended to his congregation and should urge them to use. There should be Missions and Retreats from time to time, special Services in Lent and Holy Week and an always open Church, in which the Blessed Sacrament is reserved, before which people should be taught to come and pray. The Parish Priest who freely gives himself and who diligently sees that his people are offered *all* of the blessings and privileges of their holy religion may well merit the words of the Psalmist, *"He fed them with a faithful and true heart and ruled them prudently with all his power."*

One of the responsibilities of the Clergy is the supervision of the music and directly, or indirectly, to give instructions as to what is to be sung and how it is to be sung. Too often all of this is left to the Choirmaster or Organist and sometimes to that anomaly called a "Music Committee," which should never come into being! The Canon Law of the Church puts the Parish Priest or Rector in charge of the music and defines it as a duty for him to choose what is to be sung, to call upon such assistance as he may wish, to suppress all light and unseemly music and all irreverence in the performance of the same. The Choirmaster or Organist, while engaged by the Vestry, is approved by the Parish Priest and should follow *his* counsels and directions. In some cases the Clergy themselves are either musicians or possessed of a musical sense and knowledge. In other instances they may know little about the matter further than what constitutes seemliness and good taste. Consequently, in most well-run parishes, there will be an amicable arrangement agreed upon between the Parish Priest or Rector and the Choirmaster or Organist, in which the technical rendering will be largely left to the latter, and the music sung either selected by the Parish Priest or submitted to him for approval. This sensible solution generally leads to complete and courteous cooperation and resultant good music.

Religious music is quite different from secular, for its primary purpose is the praise of God, not the pleasing of the people. Unfortunately, religious persons do not always understand what religious music is, partly due to a lack of spiritual development. In a way, appreciation of the best Church music comes by means of education, the hearing and understanding of truly religious music and the reverent and artistic rendering of the same.

Sentimental tunes, subjective hymns, florid anthems and flowery masses may delight the fancy of some persons, but *they are not religious music*. They do not express the true spirit of worship, they do not move and inspire the heart and soul. Very different is really good music. There may be allowable differences of opinion regarding the respective claims of the advocates of Masses sung in harmony or in unison, between the ancient Plain Song Masses and the beautiful music of Gounod, Schubert, Mozart and the English composers, between Anglican and Gregorian Chanting, but all agree that all of this *is* really religious music, suitable for the praise of God. Even the most elaborate compositions of the above are distinguished by beauty, dignity and simplicity.

Music is a most important adjunct to worship. Its influence cannot be over-rated. Yet it is sadly marred if the rendition is poor or if it lacks that "artistry" so difficult to define, so apparent when it is found. Here is where the real skill and ability of the Priest and the Organist come into play. If they understand "tone" and "quality" and "time" and have this artistic sense, they will put forth really good, inspiring religious music, even if they have but a small organ and few voices. As a rule, the Church of England excels in the tone and quality of its voices and the technique and artistry of its organists. And no one who has heard the boys in the College Chapels of Oxford or Cambridge or the great organ on a Sunday afternoon in Nôtre Dame, Paris, will ever forget the memory!

X

THE DEVOTIONAL LIFE OF A PRIEST

THE DEVOTIONAL LIFE of a Priest is something quite apart from the public Services in Church whether they be the Mass or the Divine Offices. The public Services are the collective offering to God of the Priest and people together in their daily round of praise and thanksgiving. The private devotions are those of the Priest alone, in his individual spiritual relationship with God. They are supplemental to the offering of the Church.

It should go without saying that "the Man of God" should be a man of prayer. This is inherent in his Sacred Office. Even in an age of rush and bustle and manifold activities, with so many different duties calling for attention, there is no excuse for the neglect of personal prayer, intercession and meditation. In his rule of life, the Priest should arrange for his private devotions. He must not be like the small boy in the story who looks at a card of printed prayers and says, "those are my sentiments," or rush through his devotions formally and mechanically, as the man in the far East turns a prayer rattle. The Priest must find *time* to pray, must *love* to pray and must pray *devoutly*.

From a practical point of view, the devotional life of a Priest is absolutely necessary to really effective work on truly spiritual and religious lines. He must realize his dependence upon Almighty God and the ever present need of Divine help and guidance. And from experience, the faithful Priest knows that the grace, power, guidance and illumination which have made him blessed and successful in his labours, have come mainly in response to prayer and Sacraments.

Then, too, he will realize that he cannot properly teach his people to pray, if he does not practice that which he preaches. As one cannot give out that which has not been taken in, a Priest cannot tell others how to pray effectually unless he, himself, has so learned and practiced. To show others the art and science of prayer and the conditions governing prayer, the Priest must know not only from the teaching given him, but also from spiritual experience. From this he will be able to tell his people that the primary purposes of prayer are: (1) to put oneself in spiritual union with God and be conscious of His Presence; (2) to worship, adore, praise, live and enjoy God and thank Him for His Glory, His Goodness and His manifold blessings; (3) to follow the example of Our Blessed Lord, Who passed all night in prayer, "the prayer of a Righteous Man that availeth much"; (4) to offer oneself to God to be used to His Honour and Glory and to learn to conform one's will to the will of God; (5) to make intercessions for "all sorts and conditions of men"; (6) to ask for grace and guidance in one's particular life and work; and (7) to ask for such things as one needs or desires according to the Mind of God. This is the way to pray and this the Priest must have learned and practiced before he can pass it on to others.

In this practice of prayer, one must remember that we do not know God's Will or that which is best or how our prayers fit in with those of others, or if they conflict with the laws which God has ordained, or what are the conditions upon which our petitions will be answered. In short, Clergy and Laity alike must realize that they do not know the Mind or Will of God, and must always pray desiring to conform to both. Given such desire, one may be reasonably sure of such Divine guidance that there will be wonderful answers to faithful and persevering prayer, made in faith, love and humility and in a state of Grace. While one never prays to change God's Will, or to alter God's Laws, in our human limitations, we do not fully understand either and should leave all issues to God, never forgetting, as the poet says: *"More things are wrought by prayer than this world dreams of."*

It is also the devout practice of many of the Clergy to make what is called a "daily meditation." This may be done in many ways, by concentration of thought upon some phase of Our Lord's Life or Work, by prayerful reflection upon certain virtues, graces or holy practices, or by taking a text or passage of Scripture and meditating upon its meaning and application.

In the olden days, the prayers of the Clergy, both secular and Religious, were more or less often coupled with ascetic practices. Some would pray with arms outstretched, so that the body formed a cross, some would lie on the cold ground or sanded floor, also with outstretched arms. Some would spend hours before a Crucifix or Sacred Relic, sometimes interrupting their prayers for bodily mortification.

Today, the ways of life and the trend of thought are so changed that the good, as well as the evil of these old time practices no longer obtains. Yet, if saner methods of devotion are followed, it might be well if the true spirit of sacrifice and bodily mastery could be retained.

In this devotional life of a Priest there should also be given time for reading and study. While all of the Clergy can hardly be expected to be men of deep learning, they should at least be well grounded in Scripture, Theology and Liturgics. It is also desirable that they have some knowledge of Art, Architecture and Music, for they frequently have to pass judgment upon additions or appointments of a Church and the character of the music. (If the Clergy generally had even this superficial knowledge, the Church would be spared some of the atrocious caricatures of ecclesiastical art and architecture and some of the utterly unsuitable music used in the praises of God!)

In this daily devotional life of a Priest, the details will properly be arranged by himself, for it is his private, personal approach to Almighty God. He will naturally, however, have recourse to the oft given counsels of those who have served as guides in the spiritual life, remembering three things specially: (1) the stimulus and inspiration of a daily meditation; (2) the joy and privilege of earnest daily intercessions for all sorts and conditions of men; (3) the peace and happiness which come from daily devotion paid to Our Blessed Lord. Thus the devotional life of a Priest not only adds to the Glory of God, but honours Christ, helps the Church, benefits the world and develops in his own being that *"beauty of holiness without which none can see God."* On his knees are won many battles. On his knees come the strength and guidance for his "cure of Souls." *"As is the Priest, so are the people,"* saith the Scriptures. The Clergy may well remember this and make the remembrance arouse a sense of responsibility, that being a prayerful Priest, he may have a prayerful people.

Those persons are greatly mistaken who think that the life of a faithful Priest is "easy." It may *look* easy because it is generally free from manual labour. Yet it *is* hard and the true Priest loves it to be so because thus, in some little measure, he may follow along in the footsteps of the Master.

The inner life of the Priest is, of course, known only to himself, to God, and to some little degree to his Confessor. He is human, as are all men and women. He has his temptations and his trials, his battles and his struggles, his times of elation and his times of discouragement, different perhaps from those of the laity, but very real. He must forget his likes and his dislikes, he must see in every soul, even that of the most sinful or disagreeable, the child of God, one made in the Image of God, after His Likeness, to be ministered to as to Christ his Lord. Tired, mind or body, he must keep his Rule. Busy with many things, he must find time for Mass, for the Offices and for Private Prayer and Meditation. He must be a devout student of Scripture and a diligent reader of works of Theology and of subjects pertinent to his duties. And he must face everything with a cheerful courage, a firm faith, a smiling face, always glad to carry on, sometimes under great difficulty. Yet while his life is a hard one, a faithful servant of God loves it and feels a warrior's joy in the conflict with the powers of Evil, knowing that Victory is always there in the end.

With the Clergy, as with others, life has many disappointments. One's efforts fail. One's ideals seem unattainable. So many unexpected things turn up. People are so unstable. The best laid plans come to naught. The dreams do not come true. Shadows darken the sunshine in the picture. Yet here is just where the faith and trust of the Priest should be triumphant, here is just where he must have optimism drive away pessimism, for the God in Whom he trusts makes *"all things work for good to those who love the Lord,"* and in His Own time will bring victory out of defeat, success out of failure, the Priest planting the seed and leaving the results to God. And for this, through prayer, reflection, observation, perseverance and unwavering trust, there must be brought into being that hopeful, cheerful attitude of mind that shows in a smiling, happy face. Natural or cultivated, the smiling face is a benediction to all. The sober face, the grave face, the worried face, the face that seems to show the burden of the world's troubles, the frowning face, may be natural, but it will never win out, cheer, comfort, attract, as the face of one who, amidst all the doubts and difficulties, trials and troubles, disappointments and discouragements of life, keeps a sunny disposition and a happy smile.

The following is offered as a suggested "Rule of Life," that may be helpful to "the Man of God":

(1) believe and practice all that the Church teaches as to Doctrine, Discipline and Worship

and always acknowledge the Authority of the Church;

(2) try to say Mass daily and be most faithful in the recital of the Divine Offices;

(3) daily offer yourself to God, saying, "O my God, I offer myself, I surrender myself, I consecrate myself with all that I am and all that I have, to be used for Thine Honour and Glory";

(4) have a definite aim and object in life, doing all to the best of your ability, for God, as in His Sight and Presence;

(5) so unite yourself with Christ in the Spirit of Sacrifice that you are always content, no matter what happens, knowing that *you always have God* and *"casting all your care upon Him for He careth for you";*

(6) cultivate detachment from earthly things, so that whether one abounds or not, one's heart is set upon the things of God, not upon the things of the world. Seek duty not happiness for then only is happiness found, and if the heart is ever lonely fill it with the love of God;

(7) think upon the shortness and uncertainty of life, at least weekly say the Office for a "holy death and merciful judgment," and look forward to "the *rest that awaiteth the people of God";*

(8) make frequent Acts of Faith, Love, Repentance and Reparation, often look at a Crucifix and think of the Passion and Death of Christ;

(9) be most faithful in Prayer, Confession and Communion; attach yourself devotedly to the

Blessed Sacrament of the Altar and make Our
Lord the center of your love and devotion;

(10) do not aim to do extraordinary things, but
rather ordinary things extraordinarily well;
remember that *"little things make perfection
but perfection is not a little thing"* and *"Whatsoever you do, do all for the Glory of God."*

And of course it goes without saying that a Priest
should never be without his Prayer Book, not only
for the reading of his Offices, if he is not in Church,
but also to be prepared for any emergency. It is a
very good thing to memorize certain Collects, Psalms
and Texts and to know by heart the form of Absolution.

It is a great joy to *see* a faithful Priest! It is a
greater joy to *be* a faithful Priest! The devotional
life, faithfully practiced, brings forth such a life,
which may be an inspiration to all: *"Behold a great
Priest, who in his day pleased God and was found
righteous."*

XI

PREACHING THE GOSPEL

PREACHING THE GOSPEL is part of the great Commission given to each Priest at Ordination. This, of course, covers all kinds of religious teaching in accord with the Word of God. Yet it is done in a different way from giving instructions. As the Church gave us the Scriptures, so the Church must expound and interpret the Scriptures and such other deposit of the Faith that has been handed down by tradition, embracing the whole content of the doctrine, discipline and worship of the Church and the duty of its members towards God and Man.

In the past were many great preachers, as for instance, Saint Chrysostom in the early Church and Saint Bernard in mediaeval times. So, too, in the eighteenth and nineteenth centuries, the pulpit saw great speakers, such as Pére Lacordaire at Nôtre Dame, Paris, Canon Liddon and Canon Knox-Little in England and many others who could be named both here and abroad.

Today, however, preaching has sadly fallen off, especially among the younger Clergy. This is very much to be regretted, for the Priest is to minister the Word as well as the Sacraments and preaching is a most important duty, never more so than today. It may be true that one may be a good Parish Priest and not a good preacher, but not being a preacher does not ensure being a good Parish Priest!

While there are some born preachers, most of the Clergy have to learn the art and science of the pulpit. Any Priest, however, properly equipped mentally and spiritually can learn to preach effectively. The first practical qualification is to have *something to say* and to know *how to say it*. One does not have to be a great scholar or theologian to speak well. In fact, the most learned are not the most fluent. Given a fair grounding in the Scriptures and in Theology, with a real message or lesson that he wishes to deliver and impart, given a fair command of his native tongue and the ability to think and speak clearly and accurately and a good Sermon is the natural consequence. The motive must be the Glory of God, the honour of Christ, the advancement of the Church and the love of Souls. A preacher must do his best and leave results to God. If earnest and sincere, he will be happy in his efforts and whether or not he sees the response, his words will never be in vain, for God ever blesses His servants when working or speaking for Him, out of the fullness of their hearts. In his preparation for preaching, a Priest should stress *"preparing himself"* rather than "his sermon." He must remember that he must *"be taking in,"* that he *"may give out."* Prayer, study and meditation must precede the sermon, in the life if not in the special preparation. With prayer, study and meditation one can preach, even if a sermon has not been prepared, but a prepared sermon will generally be fruitless if not preceded by prayer, study and meditation.

All preachers, especially successful ones, should be warned against the praise of men and also against self-laudation and self-satisfaction. Whether the talents are real or fancied, whether the Sermons are as splendid as said to be, the preacher must not put himself upon a pinnacle and think too much of his contribution to the cause of religion. For after all, in the last analysis, that which he did was through the grace, favour and assistance of God.

All preaching should be *religious* preaching, or to put it better, the preaching of Religion. The pulpit is for the preaching of the Word of God, the setting forth of the Gospel, the giving of godly counsel, the instruction in the things of God, in all that concerns the spiritual life, with accent upon the Sacraments. It is mistaken and wrong for a preacher to devote his Sermons to outside things, to the review of books, to essays on Art or Music, to polemics or politics or the things of the world. This is not his function and apart from the wrong of it, such things can better be treated by those outside the Sacred Ministry.

In the days, fortunately long since past, sermons used often to be very lengthy, it having been no rare thing for them to last from an hour to an hour and a half! One cannot but sympathize with congregations so treated! Perhaps this was that which suggested Tennyson's "Brook": "Some may come and some may go but I go on forever!" There have been those who seemed to do so!

A very good story is that of a Priest, who affected "the quiet manner" and who "did not approve of pulpit oratory." In his Church was an old lady troubled with insomnia. She had tried everything without success to induce slumber, and, as a last resource, sent for her Rector. Upon his arrival, she said to him: "O dear Father, I am so glad that you have come. You know I am so wakeful, nothing seems to help my insomnia. I thought that maybe I could sleep if you would preach to me one of your dear Sermons!"

Father Stanton, of Saint Alban's, High Holbein, London, was a wonderful preacher, not in his mode of delivery but in what he said. He appealed both to the heart and the mind and could move and convince in a most impressive way. Once at a Service was an old "Cockney" woman, who listened open-mouthed to all that Father Stanton said. At the close of the Sermon she expressed her admiration and approval by saying "Cawnt 'e chuck it off 'is chest!"

Once a preacher kept pounding the pulpit saying, "Brethren, what we need is power," repeating that again and again. One of the congregation after the service commented: "What *he* needs isn't power but ideas!" Ideas are essential for all that oratory often helps! Persuasive power is but the mode of delivering the thought.

The Church has been called an "Ecclesia docens." The Clergy should be teaching preachers. It is a mistake to think that so-called "doctrinal sermons" are not liked. On the contrary, these are the kind that are always listened to if properly preached. And doctrine does not necessarily mean the contents of the Creed. All godly counsels, setting forth moral standards and ideals, all exposition of one's duties, in Church and out, become more strong and convincing when fortified by doctrinal support and illuminating passages from Scripture. It is not doctrinal Sermons which people do not like. It is rather the vague and ineffectual way in which these truths are so often presented. To preach with persuasive power, which should ever be the aim of the Clergy, the preacher must *"read, mark, learn and inwardly digest"* that which he wishes to impart to others. Nothing counts more than the sincerity and truth of the preacher, showing his absolute personal conviction of that which he is teaching. And he must always recognize that having on his knees asked the guidance and blessing of God, he is to stand forth humbly, yet with authority, to bring God to man and man to God.

Written sermons should be avoided. In the last analysis they are nothing but essays and they lose much of their force when read out, as they generally are, in a monotonous voice. Every Priest should preach "ex tempore," in the sense, at least, that his Sermon is not written and that he speaks, in the words that come to him, or as suggested by short notes or captions. Theoretically, of course, he is guided by the Holy Spirit, Whom he has invoked, but while undoubtedly many preachers are so assisted, we must not blame God for all that comes from the pulpit in the mouth of an unprepared or unspiritually minded Priest!

To preach "ex tempore" properly involves previous thought of one's subject or text, perhaps the study of it and then the marshalling of one's ideas in an orderly, effective way. The more one understands the True Faith, the more one remembers of History, the better one is read along general lines, the better will be the Sermon. For with such equipment, error will be avoided, accurate statements will be made and at times certain subjects may be given a most picturesque, romantic and dramatic background, which holds attention and makes the matter long remembered.

Cicero once said that the three essentials to successful speaking were: *"placere, docere, movere,"* that is: *"to please, to teach, to move."* These essentials may well be applied to a Sermon, excepting that "to please" must not be allowed to accommodate oneself to approving of the evils of the day, for then it would be history repeating itself: "The prophets preach falsely and the people like it so." In striving to please the thought must rather be so to present God's Word and Will as to make it commend itself to the people's conscience and will. The preacher should declare the *"whole counsel of God,"* should set forth the doctrine, discipline and worship of the Church, should give counsel, warning, exhortation and instruction without fear or favour, with courage and conviction.

He is unworthy of his high office if he speaks in a weak or vague or compromising way; if he fails to take a definite stand for all that is right; if he fails to condemn in no uncertain words all manner of evil; if he fails to set forth the Faith as once for all delivered to the Saints and not "watered down," as sometimes done in the present day. The Priest would be untrue to his high calling if he does not say what he believes God wishes him to say, and set forth "the truth, the whole truth and nothing but the truth." It is better for him not to enter the pulpit at all rather than to presume to say that which borders upon false doctrine, heresy of schism, preached in the Name of the Father, and of the Son and of the Holy Ghost!

The reactions of the people to a Sermon are sometimes quite illuminating! Most people are interested, a few are bored, a very few try to take a nap! Those most impressed generally say little. Those who praise the Sermon enthusiastically may or may not be helped. "Actions speak louder than words" and the sequel often shows.

The preacher who speaks "ex tempore" can generally tell whether or not the people are attentive and interested; he will note the changes in many faces as his points are made or his words sink in; he will often formulate new thoughts and express new counsels, as he sees the result of that which he has just said. And while oratorical skill is often desirable, it is not an essential, particularly if the preacher has a pleasing voice, a clear utterance and some variation in intonation. It is *natural* to *love* praise. It is *wrong* to *seek* it. It is *dangerous* to *have* it. He only is safe when he seeks for the Glory of God and the good of the Souls whose spiritual life he is trying to help. Then if the praise comes, it will be rightly received, the Preacher thanking God for His guidance and giving God the glory.

XII

TEACHING THE FAITH

THE PRIEST must also be a "teacher." Preaching the Gospel and teaching the Faith are two different things, although the content is the same. The first is primarily the picturing of the life and work of Our Lord, with an application of their lessons. The second is instructing in a definite way in all those tenets, principles and truths of the Gospel as set forth by the Church.

Throughout every consideration of the Sacred Ministry, it is assumed as a fundamental requirement that those who exercise this office accept and hold all that is set forth or implied in the "True Religion."

The solemn Commission to *preach the Gospel* means not only to set forth and bear witness in a general way to the Christian Religion as taught by the Church, but also in a most definite manner to *teach* all that is comprehended by "The Faith."

This teaching of the Faith is of primary importance. It is not the presentation of religious principles, as matters of private opinion. It is the handing down of the revelation of God; the True Religion, as given by Christ to the Church, contained in the Scriptures, declared in the Creed, enshrined in the Traditions and taught by Authority. This each believer is bound to accept, for the denial of any part of this revelation puts the Soul in peril.

The teaching of the Faith consequently must be without compromise. It must clearly be set forth *"line upon line, precept upon precept, here a little, there a little,"* to include both that which is "implicit" and "explicit" in the Divine Revelation. And nothing makes a better Christian, a stronger Churchman, a more devout Catholic than the definite understanding of one's religion, of the doctrine, discipline and worship of the Church.

The Clergy, however, cannot teach effectively unless they themselves have a firm grasp and clear understanding of that which they teach. The training at Seminaries and elsewhere is all right so far as it goes, but at best it can only be superficial. After Ordination, the Clergy are expected to devote part of their time to solid reading, continuing their studies in the things of God. This is absolutely necessary if they are ever to become in any real sense theologians or scholars. It might be well if the younger Clergy would consult and be guided by some of those long time in the Ministry. For it is helpful to have this reading and study largely under the guidance of older Priests who are sound in the Faith. Otherwise, the devil may lead souls astray through many of the false modern ideas floating around today, ending in false doctrine, heresy or schism. It can never be too much stressed that the doubt and unbelief sometimes seen both in the Clergy and Laity are almost entirely due to a lack of understanding as to what the Church teaches and of the bases of such belief. The "Te Deum Laudamus" well hymns the many who through the Christian Era lived and died in the Church, holding to the Revelation of Jesus Christ. The nearer the Source, the better understood. It may well be doubted if even the most highly educated people today, Bishops, Priests, Deacons or Laymen, for all of their boasted advance, can equal the learning in *the things of God* of our forerunners in Holy Church. For the revelation given was whole and entire, unchanging and unchangeable as to content, yet ever capable of giving forth the new treasures in response to devout meditation.

In these days, when those rightly disposed are properly interested in all that concerns the public welfare and especially in that which is called "social justice," the Clergy must be on guard, lest in their enthusiasm they espouse wrong things. We refer chiefly to Communism, which rightly understood, is a system directly denying God and opposed to the Church and Religion. "Socialism" and "Communism" are two entirely different things. Without advocating the former, although along some lines it has much to commend it, we should strongly and unequivocally condemn Communism. Its advocates are clever, they present many specious arguments, they sometimes win the unwary (as for instance those called "parlour pinks") , and they have to be met with realistic opposition. It is really the old question: "God" or "Caesar," for we cannot believe in God, in Christ, in the Church, in the Christian Religion and in the individual freedom and responsibility of a soul as the child of the heavenly Father and be a Communist!

A true teacher will hold firmly to the truths he cannot understand or explain. The sometime picture of a Priest reciting the Creed and reading the Scriptures in Church, and then from the pulpit denying certain assertions he has just made in the Church's Service is a scandal. For in the last analysis it is the presumptuous assertion of a false pride, the putting oneself against the authoritative voice of the Church, which is "the *pillar and ground of truth.*" When one thinks of the mental power and the real learning of the great lights of the Church, throughout the Christian Era, who held the Faith inviolate, surely the shallow-minded modernists of today are sufficiently refuted and reproved!

It should ever be remembered that "*the Faith once delivered to the Saints*" is the revelation of God and largely comprehends holy mysteries that could not be known to man and which are beyond man's understanding. It was well said of old that "*God is from above, man is from below, God is infinite, Man is finite, and that the creature should not presume to comprehend the Creator.*" The Creed of the Church is a matter of faith, not of demonstration. It must be accepted in its entirety, without reservation, with an humble mind, realizing the impossibility of a mental grasp upon the holy mysteries of God. If this is remembered, the Clergy will find themselves devout believers and competent teachers. All of the wonderful discovery of modern science is a thing apart from religion. As a rule, science parallels religion. Where science supports the faith, it may be welcomed, although again be it said, religion is a revelation, and not needing proof. And where science seems to contradict or make difficulties, it should be disregarded as intruding in a sphere not its own. For while God wills and permits man through the use of God-given talents to learn of many of the secrets of the universe, *God only wills and permits Himself to be known* as He has revealed Himself in the Scriptures, in the Church, and in the Soul of Man. It is but foolish pride and presumption that leads some to doubt that which they cannot understand, or makes them think that Man's knowledge is superior to the mind of God or the revelation of God.

The Clergy then must ever be students, relying upon Divine guidance as to the truth. Scripture and Theology will naturally be the general lines of study. The more a Priest knows the Bible and the more familiar a Priest is with Ancient Authors, the more assurance he will have in his own belief and the more effectiveness he will have in his teaching of others. To be accurate, his belief and his teaching will have to be dogmatic, for while it is not desirable for one to confine one's thoughts or words to technical definitions, it is most necessary to think and teach in a theologically acurate way. For instance, in the presentation of such great doctrines as the Virgin Birth, the Incarnation, the Redemption, the Resurrection and the Sacraments, the Priest must realize that these are holy mysteries, above and beyond the limitations of the human mind. Nevertheless, he can and should so learn that which the Church teaches concerning them that he has a clear grasp upon them himself and so is able to impart a good understanding to others.

The Clergy today face a long list of modern works. A few are most helpful and aid in illuminating the work of the past. Most of them, however, add little or nothing to the Church's literary treasures and sometimes set forth dubious private opinions. As to older books, their name is legion, as a rule those coming from England being much superior and much more worth while than those published by American writers. The Anglo-Catholic Revival in the Church of England, in the early part of the 19th Century was prolific in splendid books for the Clergy. Many of these can still be obtained and are invaluable helps to a better understanding of the Faith and of the Anglican position.

In the Anglican Communion the need of such instruction is very great. The Roman Catholic body, with their parochial schools, their Christian Brothers and their devoted Sisters from early childhood teach religion, the Faith of the Church, and all that follows from it. Unfortunately, the Anglican Communion generally lacking day schools, and only teaching the children for a short time on Sundays in the Sunday School, with a little supplementary instruction for Confirmation, finds a people who have largely forgotten that which they learned when young and in many cases needing to be taught in many things concerning the Faith.

A most important part of teaching is the instruction of the Children. *This should be done by the Clergy.* It may seem an additional burden but it is one of the greatest opportunities and one of the greatest privileges in the ministerial life. For the children are the potential congregations of the future. Upon them, what they are and what they know, rests the welfare of the Church. During these early years, when their characters are in a formative state, they may be developed along the best lines and if they are accurately and properly taught, will rarely in later years depart far from that teaching.

The instruction of the Children should be largely *"viva voce"* in the method of the Catechism, including not only the Short Summaries in the Prayer Book, but also in all *"Such other things as a child should know for his Soul's health,"* that is to say, all that is embraced in Catholic Faith and Practice. There is no better way than the one modelled after the famous *"Method of Saint Sulpice,"* instituted in Paris many years ago by Bishop Dupanloup. Herein, in a catechetical manner, may be taught all that one should know for the intelligent practice of religion. The questions and answers may be supplemented by hymns, Scriptural Pictures and Short Talks, but the entire teaching should be by the Parish Priest or Clergy. Some things, especially definitions of doctrine, will be memorized in exact words, other things simply understood and remembered. Long elaborate leaflets or lesson papers may have their merit but they only instruct in a very vague, general way, or else touch on subjects not specially applicable to the practice of religion. The Clergy should remember that what the Children are to learn is the *Faith*, the Christian Religion: *what to believe, what to do*, setting this forth in brief but accurate and comprehensive manner, touching upon the Creed, the Prayer Book and the Bible, with special attention to the Sacramental life.

From one point of view, the subject is vast. From a more practical point of view, it becomes simplified. For while the fundamentals of religion are to be most carefully taught, that which is built upon them need only to be touched upon in a simple way. To illustrate this, in doctrine there will be special stress upon these great truths: (1) God, the Creator and Ruler of all things, with His attributes; (2) Christ: the Incarnation, the Redemption, the Resurrection, the Ascension, the Sovereignty; (3) the Holy Ghost, His Office and Work; (4) the Ministry, the Word and the Sacraments; (5) the life hereafter. These would be supplemented by simple teaching of the Sacred Scriptures, illustrated by Bible Pictures and perhaps a reference to certain great events and certain great personages in Church History. Then there would be instruction on how properly to offer Prayer, Praise and Worship, with an explanation of the principles of Ritual and Ceremonial and the appointments or Vestments of the Church and Clergy. And then the showing how to prepare and receive the Sacraments, how to make their Confessions and Communions, how to follow the Mass and other Services, how to use a Book of Devotion, also teaching them to know by heart the Lord's Prayer, the Hail Mary, the Gloria Patri, the Creed, the Commandments and Acts of Faith, Love, Repentance, Offering, etc.

Some of this, of course, may be done by the Sisters, if such work in a Parish or by certain well-instructed lay people, but they will never be able to do it as effectively as a Priest, if he has trained himself to teach. Every Parish Priest, even if alone, should try to arrange to do this most important and valuable work. "Where there's a will, there's a way," and for all of the strain of services, the Priest will find that he will have the strength given to do this. It *is* hard work; it calls for real devotion, it taxes one's powers, it means self-sacrifice, but it more than repays, for it does one of the most important things in the Church: *it teaches the children and makes instructed people.*

Many of the Clergy have been very careless about the teaching of the Confirmation Classes. Apparently they have been content with the Church Catechism of the Prayer Book, which, at best, is only what may be called "an irreducible minimum." They have forgotten the injunction in the Baptismal Office of instructing in *"all other things which a Christian ought to know and believe to his soul's health."* These latter are much more than is comprehended in the Church Catechism. The Clergy should diligently teach the Faith.

XIII

HEARING CONFESSIONS

A MOST IMPORTANT part of the duty of the Clergy is that of the Confessional. As *"the Ambassador of God"* and *"the Minister of reconciliation,"* he acts for Our Blessed Lord and forgives through His power. It is the duty of every Parish Priest to hear Confessions and to give Absolution, hereby restoring the souls of the penitents to "a state of Grace." To do this properly necessitates having public hours in Church for this purpose and the announcement of these hours, so that all may know. The people are entitled to the privilege of this Sacrament of Penance. It is not and should never be made a matter of argument or of Churchmanship. The Priest, if he is faithful to his high office, will not fail to give the people ample opportunity. For the solemn Commission of the Church received by the Priest at Ordination was: *"Receive ye the Holy Ghost for the Office and Work of a Priest in the Church of God, now committed unto thee by the Imposition of our hands: whose sins thou dost forgive, they are forgiven and whose sins thou dost retain they are retained. And be thou a faithful Dispenser of the Word of God and of the Holy Sacraments, in the Name of the Father and of the Son and of the Holy Ghost."* Nothing could be more definite or explicit than these words, and a Priest must have a much twisted mind who in the face of such a charge could excuse himself from such a plain duty! In the face of this, it is presumption for any Priest to refuse to officiate at the Sacrament of Penance. Whether he likes or dislikes the duty, whether he thinks it helpful or not, it is by Christ's command, it is a *duty*.

The history of Penance seems to show that it was the custom from the very beginning of the Church. Apparently at first, the Confessions were made openly, then on account of the possible scandal, secret or Auricular Confession was appointed, which has ever since been the general use. At the Reformation, the Anglican Communion in no way discouraged this. Rather did it accentuate it by introducing into Matins and Evensong a secondary form, not of direct Confession and Absolution, but practically prayers, owning a "State of Sin" and promising pardon, and by implication pointing to real Penance by the words *"hath given power and commandment to His Ministers to declare and pronounce to His people being penitent the Absolution and Remission of their Sins."*

Where possible, there should be the traditional Confessional, where the Priest sits in Surplice, Stole and Biretta, separated by a screen or curtain from the Penitent, who kneels on a "prieux-Dieu." A chair and a kneeling stool with screen can be similarly arranged, or if no better facilities can be had, then the Priest can sit in a pew and the Penitent kneel in the one back of him, always remembering to guard against the Confession being overheard. As a rule, Confessions should never be made in the

Sacristy, or if there is some compelling reason for so doing, the door should be left open.

The Priest will often find the time in the Confessional very tiring and wearing, especially in the very much longer hours before great Fasts and Festivals. Sometimes he will weary of the repetition of giving similar counsel when Penitents follow one another, confessing almost the same sins. Sometimes he will be startled by some revelation of wrongdoing of a grave nature. Occasionally he will be shocked by a confession of a revolting kind. In all cases, he must ever remember that he acts for Him Who is the Divine Healer, Who sent him to minister in His Name, Who said, *"As the Father hath sent Me, so send I you."* So he will see in the greatest sinner the Soul Christ wishes to save, the sheep that has strayed far from the fold, and do all he can to bind up the broken-hearted, to bring peace to the troubled heart, to turn into the right road, to lead into the paths of righteousness; to *bring them to God* and *to bring God to them.* His will be a blessed privilege, for many a Priest well knows how great sinners have become great Saints, how many have been fully rehabilitated and made splendid men and women, who would have been ruined if the world knew what they had done but whose wrongdoing was only known to God, to the Priest and to themselves.

The majority of Confessions, however, are of those who are trying to live good lives and who know that they receive the light and strength to do so chiefly through Confession and Communion. While these use the Sacrament of Penance regularly—and it is a good rule never to go less frequently than once a month—their Confessions are not to be regarded as

mere routine, or as formal or mechanical. On the
contrary, the more frequently one goes to Confession, generally the better the Confession is. The
going is at once a proof of being sorry for one's sins
and a reparation made to God for them. And as
the Priest gives the Absolution, he must think of
those Souls as precious in God's Sight, and look upon
them no longer as sinners but as those restored to a
state of grace, through Christ's Own Power of Absolution, ministered by His chosen and commissioned
representatives.

The Clergy must not only hear Confessions, they
should also teach people how to make Confessions.
And it is assumed that no Priest teaches others or
hears others, who does not humbly and faithfully
make his own Confessions to another Priest. The
more penance affects his own life in helping with
Communion to develop the "beauty of holiness" or
personal self-sanctification, the more such a Priest
will be able to help others. He will tell the people
of the special truths relating to Penance: (1) that
by Christ's Appointment, it is God's Way to seek
pardon and forgiveness; (2) that the Absolution is
of Our Lord's, coming through His Priest, since
God alone forgives sin; (3) that the Confession must
be made in sincerity and in truth, holding nothing
back, for doing so would be sacrilege; (4) that there
must be Faith, Love and Repentance, with the intention of *"having in the heart Contrition, in the
mouth Confession, in the life Amendment"*; (5) and
that the Confession is made *"under the Seal,"* not to
be known or mentioned to anyone save the Priest
and the Penitent, and this only in the Confessional.

The Priest will also teach the people how to examine their consciences, how to use a book of devotion, and how, in their confessions, only to mention the sin by name, without reference to any place or person or circumstance connected with it.

The Confessions should be short, clear and direct, mentioning simply the sins. And the people should be told *not* to write their "Sins" on paper. The writer remembers a little girl, who, coming to the Confessional, suddenly got up, and darted off, saying: "I'll be back in a moment! I left my sins in the Pew!"

The young trained to Confesson, if faithful in their later life, will show the great benefit of this wonderful sacrament, instituted by Our Lord for the health and healing of Souls. The greatest offenders of the religious and moral law are generally those never trained in Catholic Faith and Practice, who do not really know the Sacramental life.

Of course, God knows the sins before they are confessed, but it is God's way to grant Absolution as He grants other blessings through the ministry of the Church. For one to say that he can kneel down on his knees at home and ask God to forgive him and be assured of pardon, is contrary to the way God generally works. While no one should presume to limit God's forgiveness, nevertheless, if one has to be baptized, confirmed or receive the Holy Communion through the ministrations of the Clergy, why would an exception be made in the matter of Confession and Absolution! The twentieth chapter of the Gospel of Saint John and the Commission to the Priest in the Ordination Service are a complete refutation of the assumption that the normal way to pardon and forgiveness is any other than that of penance or auricular Confession and Absolution. And this Sacrament is not only for use in grave spiritual crises or in the case of special sins. It is rather to be used regularly by Priest and People, as a means of grace and for the strengthening of the spiritual life. As regular bathing and eating are essential to physical well-being, so Confession and Communion are necessary to spiritual health.

The Priest in his position of Confessor should be properly read and trained in moral theology and, incidentally, to have at least some understanding of philosophy and psychology. Like a physician, he must recognize symptoms, for many Confessions of but minor sins show trends that might well lead to grave offences. The Priest should be well taught in the various ways in which the Commandments of God are broken, how the rules and regulations of religion are disregarded, how the Church is disobeyed and how offences are either Mortal Sins or Venial Sins and fall into different divisions. Where it is necessary, he should point these out. He is not to preach a sort of a short sermon to the penitent, but simply to give godly counsel. He is not to ask questions except in very exceptional cases, where the sin has not been confessed in sufficient clearness. Sometimes, especially with the young, hardly any Counsel is required, the Penance and the Absolution being sufficient.

In the course of one's ministry, those of the Clergy who regularly hear Confessions, will have penitents who have committed grave offences, such as drunkenness, dishonesty, adultery and other sins of immorality. Naturally, these sins cannot be treated in the same way as those of less gravity. There must be some real assurance of true penitence and the penances set, even if still inadequate, must be much more than the nominal ones given for minor offences, such as saying a psalm, a few Collects, the Lord's Prayer and the Hail Mary. The penances should be remedial, in the way of reparation and satisfaction, and the counsel such as will help to rehabilitate the offender and insure future well-doing. Only very occasionally should the Absolution be deferred or given conditionally, when the Priest is not assured of proper penitence or recognition of the gravity of the offence. When possible, it is better to give the Absolution. One must always remember to receive the penitent in the spirit of charity as befitteth the Priest who ministers as the representative of the God of love and mercy.

The Clergy should study as to the proper penances to give. This, of course, will largely depend on the kinds of wrong-doing confessed and upon the age and character of those confessing. In bygone ages the penances were very real and often severe, really related to the sins. Now, however, they are usually only of a simple or nominal nature. It is well to have the penance, no matter how slight, fully understood. The writer remembers a little boy to whom, amongst other things, he gave the 27th Psalm, and going to him after seeing him kneeling a long time at his seat, found that the boy thought he had been told to read *twenty-seven Psalms!*

Counsel should largely be given in general terms. It is better to refer to a sin confessed as "*a* sin," rather than "*your* sin." Often there is no need of referring to it at all, as if the sin is not very grave, the Confession of it shows that it is recognized as wrong.

It is helpful, however, to stress "sins of omission," and teach people to confess "I have not loved God as much as I should," "I have not feared to offend God," "I have not remembered God's Presence, that He always sees me," "I have not been sorry enough for my sins," all of which is a good foundation for real repentance in other ways. One caution for the Priest hearing Confessions is not to be led into giving too specific counsel or advice on some of the matters submitted to him. Often they are more or less personal with the penitent, who, being human, may try to gain support of something upon which the Priest would advise quite differently if he knew all of the conditions or circumstances and not only as represented to him in the confessional. It is well, also, to speak with a certain reserve, although the Priest, if a gentleman and one of refinement, may discuss, should it be really necessary, the most intimate and delicate subjects without confusion or embarrassment to the penitent. It should never be forgotten, however, that the Confessional is for Confession, not for consultations. These consultations had better be at some other time, in which the Priest should be trusted, in confidence. He should be balanced in his judgments, impartial in his opinions and wise in his counsels. It is true that "in the multitude of counsel there is wisdom," but this presupposes that it is *good* counsel given by those competent to speak in the matter in question. As a rule the godly counsel of one's Parish Priest is safer, more helpful and much to be preferred than the usual advice received when many persons are consulted.

XIV

VISITING THE SICK

IT IS THE BOUNDEN DUTY of the Parish Priest to look after the sick within his "Cure." Like the Doctor, he must not be afraid of contagion or infection, but of course should use reasonable precautions in certain cases. It would be an unworthy Priest or Physician who would fail in this duty of visiting the sick and as a matter of experience, very rarely is there any real danger.

Very often sickness gives the chance of intimately helping a soul to a spiritual awakening or to a more faithful practice of religion. The Clergy should be notified of serious illness. If not and he learns it in other ways, the Priest should call. His ministrations should be cheerfully rendered and his manner such that he brings with him cheer, courage and sunshine. He should try to make the sick one resigned to the Will of God, resolved to do all possible to cooperate with the means taken for his cure and offer his illness to God for His Blessing. The patient should be persuaded to make his Confession and receive the Communion. When critically ill he should be Anointed as either a means to recovery or a preparation for death. If restored to health he should be sure to offer a Thanksgiving. Thus sickness may be made to convey a spiritual blessing and sanctify the home and all who dwell therein.

Often, however, those who are ill are not seen in the home but in a hospital. This is a little world by itself, a little world of pain and suffering and death, in which love and sympathy play a large part and in which the ministrations of religion are beyond price.

A visit to a hospital should be of great spiritual value to a Priest. He should feel what a privilege it is to minister there and his contacts should help in the beautifying of his own character. He sees so much, he learns so much and as a consequence will be called upon to give out so much as a true "Man of God." And in giving, he will be receiving, in the joy of ministration with its many spiritual lessons. For God seems very near and the Priest cannot but see how suffering bravely borne unites one with Our Lord in His suffering on the Cross. And when the Priest gives the Last Sacraments to someone dying, he senses that he is speeding that soul to the Seat of Judgment, fortified with the Bread of Life.

There is needed, however, a special approach, in the visiting of the sick or dying in the homes or hospital. One must be serious, of course, but this must never show in a glum face or a gloomy manner, or in a distant attitude towards doctors or nurses, or in a solemn greeting of the patient. One who acts like this had better stay away. He would be a depressant! And, on the other hand, boisterous "camaradie" in a sickroom is deplorable. A noisy greeting brings neither cheer nor comfort. Given, however, a bright and smiling face, a kind and sympathetic manner, a quiet and soft voice, and a few words of counsel to carry on courageously and religiously and the Priest will see the benefit of his ministrations and his visits will be gladly welcomed by patient, doctors and nurses. Those not accustomed to visit hospitals have no idea how gladly the sick welcome the Clergy and long for and look forward to their ministrations!

As hospitals minister to all, regardless of creed or colour, so Clergy of varying religions visit as called upon. A few hospitals have resident Chaplains or Chaplains who regularly make the rounds, so to speak. Unfortunately, too often the Chaplains appointed are not the proper persons for the work for they do not understand the right way to minister, and fail to give the Sacraments, as the greatest means of grace. A Priest, however, who is truly consecrated to this work, will feel that each ministration to the most humble of patients is as a ministration to our Blessed Lord Himself, and so wherever he moves through the wards he will carry joy and sunshine with him, and through hearing Confession and giving Communion, bring that *"peace past understanding."*

Trained nurses are entitled to the greatest consideration and respect, whether they enter the calling as a career or whether from a nobler motive, as an opportunity of serving the sick and dying. Trained nurses really work so hard, and their duties are so exacting, especially in hospitals, between the study of their profession and the performance of their duties! And when there are difficult cases, requiring the greatest care and entailing the greatest responsibility, how splendidly most of the nurses respond to the need! They seem true angels of mercy, as in their white or striped uniform and cap they move quickly here and there, patient and tireless in their labours, bringing hope and comfort to the sick and often seeing them leaving later on, restored to health.

In his many visits to many hospitals, the writer has always met with the most marked courtesy and consideration from doctors and nurses alike, and has seen everything done to help and facilitate his ministrations to the sick or dying. Many a lesson has he learned and many an inspiration has he carried away from those places so hallowed by the loving and merciful care of the sick and the suffering.

Ofttimes the Priest receives a call to a hospital in the late evening hours and reaches there long after dark. The lights are dimmed in the wards. A silence seems to reign, save for an occasional moan of someone in pain. In the stillness, the Priest approaches the one to whom he has been sent for to minister. Death is approaching and the minutes are few. The patient senses that his sickness is nearing its close and his eyes are pleadingly fixed upon the Priest. A whispered Confession, a last Communion, a few special prayers, a few words of counsel, then as the end approaches, the committal of the Soul to God. And the Priest, sad, yet glad over a soul in a state of grace going to its rest, leaves the body to the nurses, who care for all that was mortal.

One night the writer was called to a hospital to see one of his parishioners who had contracted pneumonia. It was getting on towards midnight. The patient was in a small ward with three other women, all having pneumonia, one very ill in an oxygen tent. The room was very close, although all three windows were open, and it was very dimly lighted, as few lamps were burning. The attendant nurse insisted upon my putting on the linen coat and linen headpiece. I ministered to my parishioner as best I could and was about to leave when a voice from the next bed said weakly: "O Father, Father, please come here!" The woman was unknown to me, but the poor soul wished a little cheer and comfort and seemed so much more contented after I said a prayer and gave her a blessing! As I left her and was again making for the door, the woman taking the oxygen sent for me. She was gasping for her breath and begged me to pray for her. She followed the words most intently and devoutly and signed herself with the Cross at my blessing. She died that night, and my parishioner the day following. I never heard what happened to the other two women, but was impressed with how those brought up in the faith so desire the benefits of religion. Very different, however, are the sickbeds and the death-beds of the irreligious from those who have their hold on God!

Quite a long time ago, one of our Servers at the Altar, who was engaged to be married, died in a hospital, following an unsuccessful operation for appendicitis. He had been a very faithful and religious young man. After receiving most reverently the Last Rites, he took all by the hand, one by one, thanking them and saying some loving word to each one. It was sad to see him go, but one could not but feel the inspiration of a holy death! *"Blessed are the dead who die in the Lord."*

As I was leaving the bedside, a nurse touched my arm and said: "Father, there is a man over there who wants to see you." I went where the nurse pointed and found a stranger to me, who was terribly upset, and much frightened, at the death of my parishioner on the other side of the ward. He had been told he could not live over ten days. "But I can't die!" he said. He had not been a bad man, had been sober,

moral and honest, but for years had paid no attention
to religion, not even to saying his prayers. Facing
death, he was afraid of God and of God's judgments!
While he had no claims on me he had a soul and no
one was looking after it. I felt that this was a plain
call of duty. So I visited him a number of times
before his death, tried to teach him the True Religion, to move him to faith, love and repentance
and to give him comfort and hope. Somehow I feel
that God blessed my efforts and that this poor troubled soul went to his rest, happier and better prepared by my ministrations.

Death and Burial in a Parish call for the deep sympathy of a Parish Priest who really has his heart in
his work and feels a sincere love for the people committed to his charge. As a minister of God he should
not spare himself to ensure as far as possible that one
dying is in a state of grace, is properly prepared to
go and has the comfort and help of the Last Sacraments. He should pray that the faithful may have a
happy and holy death and a merciful judgment, and
in his last visits to the dying, he should do all that he
can to add light and cheer and gladness to the coming end. Although he cannot but feel deep sympathy
for those who lose those they love, he should try to
make them bravely and resignedly accept their sorrow and trial, and, forgetting themselves, think only
of the *"rest that awaiteth the people of God,"* their
dear ones. It is indeed a privilege for a faithful
Priest to share in this way the sorrows of his people
and by kind and helpful words assist them in carrying
on, but it is a severe drain upon his sympathy and
strength.

XV

REMEMBRANCE OF THE POOR

THE CHURCH THROUGHOUT her history, with rare exceptions, has always espoused the cause of the poor and oppressed. The Clergy are to be no respecters of persons, but to see in them souls precious to Almighty God.

The Parish Priest should always be willing to see those who appeal for help at his door. Organized charities are supposed to care for all of those in distress, and all in all they do a good work and minister faithfully according to their ability. Yet everyone knows that they are somewhat slow of action, sometimes unnecessarily strict and through their experience become rather difficult to persuade to help in many cases. Often those who call upon the Clergy are in great distress, their conditions emergency ones, and they need immediate help or counsel. It seems heartless to turn them away and the Priest, whose office is the extension of Our Lord's work on earth, should feel that it is both a duty and a privilege to minister in His Name to these poor unfortunates.

If receiving a good salary (which is extremely rare!) or possessed of an outside income (also extremely rare!), he can do much in assisting financially those who appeal for help. If, however (as is most generally the case), his stipend is so small that it is a struggle to live on it, he cannot be expected to aid with money, but he can show sympathy and give counsel which may be of great cheer and encouragement to the "down and out." Like the Apostles, the Priest may say "silver and gold have I none," and yet, without working a miracle, by a smile, a few words of advice and a little friendly sympathy he can send away the caller with a lightened heart.

A Priest readily knows the good from the bad, the deserving from the undeserving and is rarely deceived. Sometimes, when others think that he is being imposed upon, he is but taking his chances open-eyed, with some poor unfortunate, even as did the good Bishop in Victor Hugo's "Les Miserables." Sometimes kind words may be as helpful as money, and the Priest may be able to bring the needy person in contact with those who can help in a more practical manner. Of the callers, some are in search of work, some have sickness at home, some need hospital treatment, some have houses with no coal to heat them, some have families needing food, some are simply hard up. And of these, there are some who have never before asked help and in their need would rather appeal to the Clergy than to Organized Charity, for often it is but innate self-respect on the part of a really unfortunate, but deserving person, to refuse to be "investigated." Often have the Clergy known their counsel not only to lead to practical help, but also to complete rehabilitation. They may be able to give little, but given in the Name of Christ, it "benefits three": Our Lord, the unfortunate person, and the Priest who gives.

Often, too, a few religious counsels may be given, irrespective of the belief of the one addressed. Who can know if they have not frequently resulted in a careless or unchurched person again going to worship, or saying his prayers, or perhaps even seeking the Sacraments! All of the Clergy know that this happens, if not always, at least from time to time. And sometimes, the questioning has its humorous side, when the one asked as to his religion looks the Priest over, as if trying to find a good answer!

In being accessible to those in need, the Clergy become familiar with many phases of life, with which they would hardly meet in their own Parishes. They learn much of the problems and difficulties, of the trials and troubles of the very poor, they come in touch with the unemployable as much as with the unemployed; they begin to sense that struggle for subsistence of those sometimes called "the submerged tenth," and see life from many different angles. A good Priest, a true "Man of God," thus grows in kindness, in sympathy, in understanding, and he ever becomes a better Priest and a better man from these contacts with "all sorts and conditions of men."

In referring to religion with the tramp or man at the door, one, of course, does not preach or lecture or proselyte. He simply refers to religion as a duty and as a means of pleasing God and getting His blessing and protection. The counsel is but a general one, to remember and practice one's religious duties and go to whatever Church he belongs to. When asked why they have gotten careless about Church, like those in the Parable, generally, "they all with one consent begin to make excuse." They "did not have fit clothes," "they had no money for the collection!" "they had moved away from where they used to go," "they would feel strange in a new place," and so on "ad infinitum." Almost always they seem ashamed of themselves and frankly own their fault in that they no longer practiced their religion.

The Parish Priest also has amusing experiences. Charity has its brighter side and some of those appealing for aid are interesting or attractive characters. A few incidents may be entertaining and illustrative. A very respectable elderly man, who had asked for help had no teeth. The writer sent him to the City Mission and asked their cooperation, but was told that they did not consider their charities to "cover teeth for indigents." After much persuasion, those at the City Mission, who had always been most helpful, consented and arranged to go "fifty-fifty" with the writer and have the Episcopal Hospital do the work. About a month later, the author said to a man at the door, "Where are your teeth? Didn't the Mission ever give you your teeth?" "No," he said, "I never got any teeth from the City Mission!" Quite provoked, the man was sent to the Mission with a letter faulting them for not keeping their promise. In about an hour the telephone rang and a voice said, "We gave your man the teeth. This fellow today is another chap!" One may imagine the mix-up, but the sequel was satisfactory, for again, after very much persuasion, and an appeal to their sympathy, we again went fifty-fifty and this second man was adorned and made very happy with his set of teeth! Not many of the Clergy have been so successful in having teeth in their works!

During the depression it was often through the instance of the Clergy that persons delinquent in their rent had the arrears written off and new leases signed. Often a call at the door resulted in some arrangement being made with a coal dealer or provision man to cooperate and temporarily relieve the distress. It may be that in the future which some optimists picture many reforms will do away with much of the distress of today, but it is well to remember Our Lord's words *"the poor ye have always with you."*

Very often the Parish Priest will be called to minister to those who are sometimes referred to as "broken lives," who have "badly slipped in the way." He may have to call at prisons, a most depressing task except to the most hopeful and optimistic, for, alas! it is hard to believe in "prison repentance," or in the ultimate reformation of those who have come under the law, for so seldom is there seen any desire to make reparation or to live a new life. Yet the effort to reform these poor derelicts should be made and the Clergy should do their utmost, even in a "forlorn hope." The greatest difficulty is to bring about a realization of sin and the need of a real repentance. Too often, the attitude of the offender is that of rebellion against his being caught and confined and the desire to get out. He is "sorry" but, strictly speaking, neither for the crime nor for the sin. Amongst the poor as with others, drinking and immorality are the two greatest causes of the downfall of people. And both are hard evils to fight, for nothing will make people win out from their temptations except their own will power. To the strengthening of this *will to do right* must be the main object of all prayer, Sacrament and godly counsel. Given this will power, the drunkards or the immoral will reform.

XVI

THE ADMINISTRATION OF A PARISH

BOTH THE CLERGY who have been ordained and those who are considering taking Holy Orders should know about the relationship of a Priest with his Parish. It is in no way like that of a Sectarian Minister, who is engaged or employed by the ecclesiastical body, to which he belongs. The Priest is "called" by the Congregation, or "Sent" by the Bishop to assume charge of a Parish, to become its *head* and to *exercise authority* over its members. This is clearly set forth in the "Office of Institution." The Priest is not accountable to the people nor under the direction of the Vestry but is solely responsible to the Church and the Bishop, subject to the Canons and Constitutions.

Consequently, the conduct of a Parish is in the control of the Rector or Priest and the Services, Meetings and Organizations should be such as he approves and authorizes. If his rights and responsibilities are clearly comprehended by both Priest and People, his authority will be acknowledged and most friendly and peaceful relations will prevail, with mutual regard and respect. It should be the desire and aim of both the Vestry and the Congregation to act in accordance with their Rector's wishes and counsels and in every way to cooperate with his ideals and policies. And the Priest, on his part, remembering his responsibility of watching for their souls as one who must give account to God, should always try to be a devoted Pastor, a true Shepherd of his sheep. Such a Parish is sure to be blessed and prospered by God.

Parishes and Peoples vary. Consequently no specific rules could be given to apply similarly to all. Yet there are some counsels that may be followed, which have been proven successful in operation in the practical experience of many Parish Priests.

One of these is to prevent a possible rivalry and jealousy, with their many misunderstandings, which comes amongst guilds and organizations through the choice of their officers by the members. As the Rector is *"ex officio"* the head of every Society, he will often find that peace and harmony will replace strife and discord if *he individually chooses and appoints* those who engage in the work of the Church, as for instance those who serve in the Altar Society or Guilds, those who act as Acolytes and Servers, and those who sing in the Choir. He should also select those who will be their officers or directors. This may not seem to be the democratic way but it should be remembered that the Church is not a democracy but a Kingdom. As a president appoints his cabinet, as a general chooses his aides, so a Parish Priest may select those who really represent him. The procedure mentioned has been most successful wherever tried, and has resulted in a far greater measure of unity and cooperation than is possible when other ways are followed.

Occasionally strained relations arise between a Parish Priest and his Vestry. This is most unfortunate, and while the Parish Priest is not always blameless, as a rule the trouble is generally due to a misunderstanding on the part of the Vestry as to the rights of the Rector. Their respective responsibilities may be referred to as the "Spiritualities" and the "Temporalities," the former being in the control of the Clergy, the latter of the Vestry. The duties and prerogatives of the Vestry are entirely secular, covering the keeping of the buildings in proper condition, the providing ways and means for raising the necessary funds for the worship and the work and the calling of a Rector or Priest, subject to the approval of the Bishop. And in all this, the Vestrymen are not to act for themselves individually but as the representatives of the Congregation collectively. They are not to interfere concerning the teaching of the Faith, the conduct of the Services, the Ceremonial of Worship, the choice of the Music or the work of the Guilds, responsibility for which is distinctly inherent in the Rector or Parish Priest.

At the meetings of the Vestry, the Rector is Chairman *"ex officio,"* and while full discussion of all proper matters should always be permitted, unless the Parish Priest suggests something obviously mistaken, a good Vestry will approve his views and accede to his wishes. As a rule the Clergy best know that which is best for the Church and Parish. While patient of the preferences and opinions of the people, the Priest should faithfully uphold the doctrine, discipline and worship of the Church and if need be assert his authority as the one responsible. Given mutual regard, affection and courtesy, however, disagreements will rarely arise. Many long pastorates prove the truth of this happy relationship often prevailing.

A most important thing in the administration of a Parish is the continuous teaching of the people in the things of God. Sometimes the Clergy are careless about this, assuming that their congregations know all that is neecssary. Nothing could be more mistaken than this, for not only are there continual changes in a Parish but also there are always those who have forgotten or who have never fully learned. And there is no excuse whatever to refrain from teaching, and to "follow the line of the least resistance," when a Congregation seems unwilling to hear or accept the True Faith. Indeed, in such a case there is a distinct duty for the Priest to set forth in a most clear and explicit way the "whole Counsel of God" as to doctrine, discipline and worship, especially stressing the Sacramental life. In fact, each year, from time to time, it is advisable to remind the people of the necessity of fasting Communion, the comfort of Confession and Absolution, the duty of abstinence on Fridays and in Lent, the keeping of the Fasts and Festivals, the proper way to worship God, and the need of self-denial, and self-discipline in the development of the Spiritual life. Generally if a Priest preaches and teaches with persuasion and power, the people will gladly follow his counsels. If sometimes he meet opposition or resistance in his setting forth of the teaching and practice of the Church, it should only redouble his resolution through prayer, patience and perseverance to convince his people and bring about their godly obedience.

Sometimes, especially in Parishes where the people have not been well taught, difficulties arise about Baptisms, Confirmations, Funerals and particularly

Marriages. With kindness these troubles, if they come, may be amicably adjusted but it is better to avoid them by previous teaching and training. In all cases, however, the Priest should conscientiously carry out the rules and regulations of the Church.

Baptisms, Confirmations, Funerals and Marriages should always take place in Church. In Baptism, three proper sponsors or godparents should be ensured, who should be communicants of the Church in good standing. If this is impossible, one may do. The baptism of the child is of primary importance, and the child should not be penalized, so to speak, for the lack of sponsors. As the Baptism generally is publicly administered, at a Service, the Priest often has the chance of giving in or before his Sermon a few words of godly counsel to the godparents as to their duties.

As has been said elsewhere, a Funeral should properly include a Requiem, which may be preceded by what is known as the Burial Office. Frequently today the Burial Office is said at the Home and the Requiem Mass said or Sung at the Church. Families which object to this in whole or in part are generally very grateful afterwards, if they have allowed themselves to follow the godly counsel of the Parish Priest and be persuaded to have the Funeral in this way.

It is in the matter of Marriage that misunderstandings often arise. Many persons have no conception of what Holy Matrimony really is. Fortunate are they, when in their Parish they have been well instructed in this as in other things, for if they know the law of God and the Church they will be glad that the Priest is careful to see it scrupulously followed. And in the little counsel he is now bidden to give to those to be married they will welcome the plain setting forth of their duties in this holy estate.

Those to be married should be told of the *purposes* of holy matrimony: the bringing children into the world, the prevention of sin, the joy of companionship. They should also be warned of the *prohibitions:* too close relationship, physical incapacity, impotence, deceit, insanity, contraint and divorce. The State regards marriage as a *"Contract"* for bed and board, but the Church holds it as a *"Union"* made in the Sight of God, which cannot be broken except by death. Both parties must have had holy Baptism, for if one is unbaptized, there is no Christian marriage since it comes within the prohibition mentioned by Saint Paul. Thus it is most important for the Priest officiating to be sure regarding the baptism of those entering Holy Matrimony.

No divorced party has the right to marry again during the life of the former partner, for divorce does not affect the mystical union for *"those whom God hath joined toegther let no man put asunder."* Neither love, nor pity, nor sympathy should allow one to forget God's law and Christ's command. Any marriages of a divorced person during the life of the former husband or wife is adultery, and no acceptance of such persons by smart society or others can do away with this plain fact. *"Be ye well assured that if any persons are joined together otherwise than as God's Word doth allow, their marriage is not lawful."* It is adultery and cuts off the offender from the Sacraments of the Church. It is hard for the Priest, sorrowing for the results of mistakes that have been made, to take a strict and definite stand here, but it is his plain duty. It will help him if he often, in referring to Holy Matrimony, gives a few words of instruction and repeats the words of the Preface to its Solemnization, that marriage must *"not by any to be entered into unadvisedly, or lightly, but reverently, discreetly, advisedly and in the fear of God."* That which is called "annulment" only applies to marriages contrary to the prohibitions, or unconsummated, when as a consequence the marriage was *"null and void ab initio."*

A conscientious Priest, resolved to uphold the Law of God as to Marriage, need not be disturbed if Canons contrary to such are ever adopted, for he cannot be required to officiate in any instance which would violate such law of God as embodied in the Book of Common Prayer.

One of the many secrets that help a Priest in making a successful Parish is to be no respecter of persons but to treat everyone with the same courtesy and consideration. He will naturally have his likes and dislikes, but he must not show them. There should be no preference in his relations with his people. Generally, he will have "all sorts and conditions of men," he will often be bothered and bored, he will have his patience severely tried, he will find it hard sometimes to control his temper, especially when tired and depressed. Yet he should bear with all, try to help all and endeavor to be a true spiritual father to every one of them. Above all, he must never discriminate on account of social position or financial ability. The most humble children of God, the most poor and lowly of the people are entitled to the same regard and consideration as the more fortunate and favoured. And the children should ever be close to his heart, for not only are they the coming strength of the Church, but also are they the most receptive of all that the Church teaches.

Given this love for the people and his fatherly devotion to all of them, he will have in return a regard and affection which will make his Parish a true spiritual home. This will be of the greatest help in his guidance of souls. Like the Centurion, he will say: *"Go and he goeth," "Come and he cometh," "Do this and he doeth it."* He will have his own authority recognized because he himself is *"one under authority"* to Christ and the Church, a true Servant of his Lord, watching for Souls *"as one that must give account"* and winning Souls. As a true Priest of the One, Holy, Catholic and Apostolic Church, he is the Spiritual father to everyone, without fear, favour or preference.

The Clergy should be particularly careful not to intrude into the field of politics. Naturally, a Priest has and should have decided political views, especially as they apply to the social well-being. He is quite within his province to try to persuade others individually to see things the same way, and on very important occasions, as in times of grave crisis, when much is at stake, he is also quite justified in speaking upon these matters from the pulpit. As a rule, however, it is better to keep his preaching free from any kind of political propaganda, for a congregation is not all of one mind, and since they are in Church to worship God, it seems like taking advantage of them for a Preacher to put forth his views where the hearers cannot set forth their own.

Social Justice, as it is sometimes spoken of, is quite a different thing and should not be associated with political parties. It is the duty of the Clergy to take a definite stand here, for Social Justice is inherent in the Gospel. The Clergy should endorse and help all movements for reform. In the Middle Ages the greatest friend of the poor and down-trodden was the Church, and today it should be the same. The Church is for all people, and as such, her Clergy should be deeply interested in the many complicated problems of the day, should definitely espouse the cause of social justice, and have the keenest sympathy with the underprivileged and the "forgotten man." Every wise movement for reform, every earnest effort for the betterment of conditions should enlist the sympathetic support of every Priest, irrespective of what might be his inclinations along party lines.

The Priest, by his words and influence, may do much to win people to help great causes, such as the elimination of the slum, the stopping of the sweating system, the prohibition of child labour troubles, and the improvement of conditions in general. This is not "politics" but rather the application of one's religion in a practical way for the betterment of the lot of the people, in furthering the ideals of "Life, Liberty and the Pursuit of Happiness."

One of the most important duties of a faithful Priest is that of visiting his poeple. No one is a true Pastor who dislikes this or who looks down upon it, if his Parish is composed of those in humble walk of life. A gentleman born is never condescending. Conscious of his own birth and breeding, he can accommodate himself to "all sorts and conditions of men" without any assumption of superiority and without any feeling of humbling himself. He sees in them his brethren and comrades, finds all of the contacts interesting and feels sorry if others are less fortunate than himself. Whatever the birth or background, the Church expects all of her Clergy to have a real interest in and a real responsibility for the Souls in their "Cures." To visit in a perfunctory way will be "love's labour lost." To call in the proper spirit, and show a real interest in their welfare will win for the Priest the affectionate regard and respect of all. He will come to know of their joys and sorrows, their successes and failures, their trials and temptations, their aims and efforts. There will be many confidences. There will be many chances for counsel and help and sympathy. Through visiting, the true Pastor or "Man of God" will find a reward for all his labours.

With those newly confirmed, it is most unfortunate that so many of the Clergy leave them alone after they have made their First Communion, apparently assuming that they will continue unwaveringly along the right path, always faithful to their religious duties. He should remember the dangers of the world, the flesh and the devil! And the very serious temptations that come in the way of the newly confirmed, young and old. They will often be associated with careless and worldly people. They will hear the Faith attacked and the Worship ridiculed. And unless encouraged and strengthened in a wise and sympathetic way, in a few years they will have succumbed to the allurements on every side and have "gone with the wind."

The Parish Priest should teach his people to live their religion by rule, not by an involved, difficult rule, but by a simple one, mainly embodying faithful attendance upon Mass, Confession and Communion, the regular saying of one's prayers and the putting into practice that which they learn and profess in the cultivation of Christian character. In all of this, especially in their youthful years, the people should have the diligent oversight and Godly counsel of the Clergy. If the minimum rule in the Parish is for the Confirmed to go to their "Duties" of Confession and Communion once a month, the Parish Priest should try to see that they do so. He can have a little list in his Prayer Book and check the names week by week as their times come. A Priest hearing confessions, whether or not he sees the penitent, generally recognizes a voice or some characteristic that tells him who is making the Confession. So he can check his list. If one is regular and faithful, a few words of recommendation and encouragement may be given at the end of a Confession. If one is careless and irregular, a little counsel or warning may be kindly and persuasively given. It helps a Priest to be a faithful Shepherd of Souls. It helps a Parishioner to know that there is such an one. Fatherly kindness is essential. Rarely is sternness necessary. And scolding is never advisable! Saint Francis de Sales used to say that "one catches more flies with sweets than with vinegar." A Parish Priest who shows a kind solicitude and a fatherly interest will be listened to. If people really love and respect their Parish Priest, there is little that they will not do for him!

Some of the Clergy, apparently, have a bad memory, both of faces and names. This is most unfortunate, for all persons like to be recognized and remembered. The following shows what is meant. A curate once greeted some young girl at the door of the Church, after the Service, saying: "I think that

we have met before. Where are you living now?"
"Father, I live just where I did last Friday night when
you called upon me!"

It is through his diligent visiting that the Priest
has the chance of advising, counselling, cautioning
and guiding. His visit must not be a mere social
contact. It must be different from any other kind of
a visit, not, of course, formal, stilted, unnatural or
over-serious, but one in which, after a bright smiling
approach, and the interchange of the usual ameni-
ties and pleasantries, sometimes a laugh and joke,
the conversation is turned to the Church and to Religion and the Priest finds the opening for what he
wishes to say along spiritual lines.

One of the great temptations to some of the Clergy
is to develope a Parish along the lines of what is called
"institutional work," the formation of all kinds of
guilds and societies, for pleasure or for profit, often
submerging the religious in the social.

Fortunately, this trend seems to be on the decline
and it is being realized that this "institutional work"
is not really the field of the Church. There are times
when a Parish, in poor circumstances, may feel that
it has to resort to dances, card parties and minstrel
shows to raise a little money against a deficit. That
may be excusable, perhaps even commendatory, in
the eyes of many, yet one cannot but think that the
money might have been freely given. In any event
there seems little reason to have these means of
entertainment simply to establish a social atmosphere
and to give pleasure. For one does not win Souls by
card parties and dances, innocent as are these enjoyments, and one does not stimulate the spiritual life
by minstrel shows, much as one may appreciate them.

And "Beer" and "Bingo" are bad ways of raising money for God!

Occasionally, perhaps, Parish "parties" may be advisable, but as a regular thing, organized as part of an institutional work, quite the contrary is the case, and the Priest who approves or permits is only wasting his time and energy upon something that does not belong to the real Cure of Souls.

It does not follow from this that a Priest should not have guilds and organizations in his Parish. These, however, should be religious guilds and organizations, generally either associated with the work of the Altar or with Missions or with the furtherance of the Spiritual life.

It is a most desirable thing for the Clergy to understand financial matters. To be a good man of business is quite an asset in a Priest and a Parish is generally much better run financially when this is the case. While the Vestry is in charge of "temporalities," the advice, counsel and wishes of the Rector figure very largely and in some Parishes are paramount and always followed. It is a most unpleasant thing for a Priest always to be appealing to his people to increase their offerings or to respond to the many diocesan demands for funds. Large and flourishing Parishes, with rich Congregations, have no conception of the difficulties of smaller Churches, in money matters. There may be a beautiful building, there may be a prosperous looking people, there may be very generous givers, according to their means, but the number of wage earners or the earning capacity of those who work may be very limited. What, with assessments for the Diocese and Episcopate, the apportionment or expectation for Missions and the extra appeals, a large part of the income is allotted before the sum for the Parish Budget can be considered. Yet the Clergy should stress the duty and privilege of giving to Church and Charity, as a real test of Religion. The greater the sacrifice, the greater the reward. Yet one's best cannot always meet all of the demands.

Few people praise enough the sacrifice on the part of many a Parish Priest, who, uncomplaining, goes on year after year with a stipend that is disgracefully small and often most irregularly paid. No wonder then if the Clergy are not good financiers, a Parish goes on the rocks.

It is helpful both to the Parish and to the Parish Clergy to have a parochial Mission at least every few years. Sometimes it may last several weeks. A ten days' Mission is very popular and generally accomplishes the aim: the spiritual stimulation of the people, the moving many to greater faith, love and repentance.

Many think of Missions as only being conducted by the "Religious." Frequently, however, there are Parish Priests who are equally successful in drawing large numbers and in securing results. They, however, must come from centers outside the Parish for, generally speaking, the Parish Clergy should never try to conduct a Mission in their own Church.

Before a Mission is arranged for, a Rector should have carefully discussed the matter with those whom he has chosen to carry out the plan. As really responsible for the souls in his charge, he should be told the general plan and procedure proposed by the Missioners and then, having approved, he should confidently and trustfully place the conduct of the Mission in their hands.

A Mission generally will aim to have both preaching and instruction, to bring those making the Mission to attend daily at Mass, and before the close of the Mission make their Confession and Communion. Exhortations will be had, godly counsels will be given, a rule of life recommended and the urging of all to have the Missionary Spirit by word and example to bring others to Church.

Then there is the need in every Parish of Retreats, one or more every year, the best times possibly being in or before the seasons of Advent and Lent. Long Retreats are not suitable to the average Parish. Those who wish to make these can generally find opportunity at some one of the monasteries. An ordinary Parish Retreat may be made in a day, preferably beginning with Mass and ending with Benediction. The people should learn by coming, the inestimable value of a Retreat, when, even apart from the devotions of the Church or the counsels of the Conductor, the *"still small voice"* of the Holy Spirit speaks to the soul. And the Clergy should always make a point of themselves attending a Retreat for Priests, for they, above all, can profit by this experience.

In all of this administration of a Parish, so different from the conduct of a business or profession, the Rector or Parish Priest must continually humbly remind himself of how he stands before God as well as the people, and must exercise his vocation or "calling" as in the sight of God.

And in this calling, the Priest must never forget, but always remember and realize that he is the Divinely chosen Agent, called to be a *"Man of God,"* who is to *"Serve the Lord Christ,"* making religion his very life, making God first, and ever seeking in his prayers guidance from above: *"Lord, what wilt Thou have me to do?"*

While the individual life and the ministerial life are two distinctly different things, the Priest should ever remember that the first must be consistent with the latter. In his ministerial life, he is the representative of Our Lord, the ambassador of God, speaking in His stead, acting in His Name. Thus every ministerial act is in reality Our Lord working through him, for Christ said, *"As the Father hath sent me, so send I you."* In Baptising, in saying Mass, in hearing Confessions, in ministering to the sick and dying, and in all other official acts, it is Our Lord ministering by and through him, so the Priest must be reverent, recollected and conscious of his responsibility. Outside of his official acts, however, his individual life is as he makes it. We know that the unworthiness of the Minister in no way affects the validity of his official acts, yet, since it is the same person who acts individually as well as ministerially, there should be a correspondence, for as Saint Paul says, *"All things are lawful, but all things are not expedient."* His conduct must be above reproach. He may be and should be bright, cheerful, happy, approachable and possessed of a sense of humour and be able to enter into the spirit of innocent enjoyment, but withal, maintaining a certain dignity that wins the respect of all. No thinking person likes or respects the Priest who masquerades in lay dress and is known as a "hail fellow well met" sort of person. They want a friend whom they can trust, a Priest who acts and speaks as "a *Man of God,*" one of strong spiritual power, one who *"walks with God."*

This is a high ideal. This embodies an exalted standard. Yet, for all the shortcomings of the Clergy (and they are many, both individually and collectively) one cannot but think that they compare favourably with their lay brethren, from which ranks every Priest comes.

When one thinks of the great commission given to those in the Sacred Ministry by Our Lord, through the Holy Catholic Church, one is overcome with wonderment as he begins to realize the truth of the words, *"we have these treasures in earthen vessels!"* We see a Priest (as any other man subject to temptation and liable to human frailty) declared to be *"the Ambassador of God";* a Priest handicapped by many limitations, yet to *"speak in Christ's stead," "in His Name";* a Priest confessing his own sins as a humble penitent yet given power and commandment to give pardon and Absolution to others; a Priest knowing his own needs and weaknesses, yet preaching the Gospel and *"declaring the whole Counsel of God";* a Priest, who feels his own littleness and unworthiness, standing at the Altar to offer in holy mystery the greatest Sacrifice in the world and through the power of Christ to consecrate Bread and Wine to be Our Lord's Body and Blood. The wonder of it all! The man of God must realize all of this, yet he must not "pose" or act as a superior sort of person. He must be natural ("human" as they say) and whenever or wherever he succeeds in being as he should be, he should give the praise to God not to himself. No wonder we are told in Scripture to *"reverence them very highly for their work's sake."*

XVII

THE "RELIGIOUS"

No BOOK upon the Sacred Ministry would be complete without a special reference to those of the Clergy known as the "Religious." These are those who in the Monastic Orders have taken the vows of Poverty, Chastity and Obedience. Their life cannot be too highly commended, or their work too highly praised. And this, without any reflection upon those others of the Clergy, or any underrating of their labours. It is not a matter of rivalry as to which most excel. It simply is a matter of vocation, for all of the Clergy are not called by God to this special sphere of Service for Him as a "Religious."

There is always a certain glamour or romance about the Monastic Orders, which have figured so largely in the history of the Church. Whether one thinks of the earliest days, when Saint Benedict founded his famous Order and Rule, or of mediaeval times, when the great Monasteries flourished and the beautiful Abbeys were built, or of the present day, when they are known far and wide through Missions and works of a most practical kind, we see a life at once consecrated in its aims and most picturesque in its expression.

In their ideal, the "Religious" give up all for God, cutting themselves off from the world, engaging in a continual round of prayer and supplementing their devotions by literary and artistic work, labour in the fields, care of the sick, ministering to the poor and espousing the cause of the oppressed, with little rest and a strict rule. The preservation of learning, the pursuance of Art, the knowledge of agriculture, the development of Architecture, the origination of the Hospital are all largely due to the Monks. If the Monastic Orders had never arisen or had ceased to be, the world would have suffered an irreparable loss.

The Monastic Orders had their faults as they had their virtues. So have all men and all organizations. Yet as one recalls the accomplishments of the "Religious" surely the virtues, not the faults stand out! As one glances at the lovely illuminated tomes and manuscripts and paintings which have come from their hands, or looks over the beautiful ruins of ancient abbeys, like Tinterne or Fountains, sleeping in their environment of forest or stream, or thinks of the poor traveller freely given the Dole of Ale and Bread at the Monastery gate, or the traveller rescued from the snows on the Grand St. Bernard, or of those who in Monasteries found sanctuary from their enemies, one must see what a tremendous power for good, for the cause of religion and humanity was found in those consecrated lives. And today, at home and abroad, while conditions and circumstances are greatly changed, the world, even that part that includes the Anglican Church, thanks God for those "Religious" who, in their midst, are carrying on the same traditions for all the altered times.

While it is quite true that the "Religious" have often sadly fallen from their high ideals, so have done the other Clergy, and it is well to remember that in most of the reforms which have followed upon these lapses, it was the "Religious" themselves who brought them about. History shows plainly that most of the criticism brought upon the Monastic Orders was from a desire to rob them of the fruits of their labours or the treasures which had come to them through devout gifts and thanksofferings. An instance of this was the suppression of the Monasteries and the appropriation of their possessions by Henry VIII and his rapacious followers. There is a story told of King Richard I, the "Lionhearted," who when accused of certain failings, said: "I have already given away these daughters in marriage: pride to the Templars, luxury to the Black Monks and avarice to the White Monks," but history will tell more of the virtues inherent in the lives of the "Religious" of that day than in the none too nobleminded King Richard! There can be little doubt that again and again it was the "Religious" who saved Christianity, it was the Monastic Orders which carried on the Faith in a "wicked and naughty world."

From the very first there were Monks, Communities and Hermits, who lived away from the cities in desert and lonely places, these more or less lacking rule and sometimes rather turbulent and undisciplined. It was Saint Benedict, early in the Sixth Century, who established Monasteries as we know them, and his rule is the basis of most of the Orders today. The Benedictines and the Augustinians (who ascribe their Rule to the great Latin Father) are the two oldest Monastic Orders. In mediaeval times the Carthusians, the Cistercians and later the Carmelites were very prominent. All of these Orders embraced amongst the brethren many of the most distinguished men of the time. The Cistercians have left a notable witness to their artistic and architectural ability in the Abbeys which they built; many of the ruins today, as those of Tinterne or Fountains, or Melrose, witnessing to that former glory and beauty.

In the thirteenth century came those Orders known as "the Preaching Friars," the Dominicans and the Franciscans, often popularly referred to as "the Black Friars" and "the Gray Friars." They were distinctly different, as their name implies, from the older Orders. Saint Francis of Assissi will always be remembered and loved. Since the earliest days, the Monastic institutions have continually multiplied. There are many Orders in the world today with varying rule.

In the Anglican Communion, Henry VIII wrecked the Monastic life in England, robbed the Monks of their possessions and ruined the Abbey Churches and Conventual Houses, distributing the lands amongst his favourites. Terribly handicapped, the Monastic spirit still survived, as shown in the life of Nicholas Ferrer and Little Gidding. In the Anglo-Catholic Revival, a restoration has taken place to some extent in the Church of England. There are flourishing Orders for men in England, such as those splendid centres at Cowley, Kelham, Mirfield, Plaistow and Pershore, where we see respectively, the "Society of Saint John the Evangelist," the "Society of the Sacred Mission," the "Community of the Resurrection," the "Society of the Divine Compassion" and the Benedictines, and in America few there are who do not know of the Order of Holy Cross and the Society of Saint John the Evangelist," familiarly spoken of as "the Cowley Fathers" and "the Holy

Cross Fathers." In the establishment at Little Portion, Mt. Sinai, Long Island, we see a revival of the
Franciscans and in the west very recently the restoration of the Benedictines. So helpful is their work that
it is most desirable that there should be a large
increase in membership in these Orders.

One does not become a "Religious" by simply
thinking that he "would like to be a Monk." It is
a question of vocation, even more to be considered
than the calling to the Sacred Ministry. The would-be
"Religious" must communicate with the Order and
follow out all of the requirements of having his "vocation" tested, especially as to his glad and willing
submission to the Rule and his obedience to authority.

As one thinks of the "Religious" in the past and
in the present, how many and varied are the pictures that come before the mind; pictures taken at
random that teach many things: Saint Anthony in
his seclusion, meditating on mortality, as he looks
on a skull; Saint Jerome in his cell at Bethlehem,
translating the Scriptures; a scribe on his knees
illuminating in gold and colour some sacred page;
a little band of Monks going out to care for suf-
ferers from the plague; a porter giving out the Dole
to some starving traveller; a Savonarola done to
death for his reforms; Fra Angelico engaged in most
lovely works of religious art; Saint Bernard going
into the forest to found the new monastery of Clairvaux, or preaching the Crusade; Saint Thomas
Aquinas, meditating upon "Who is God," "What
is God," and later writing the greatest of all theo-
logcal works, "The Summa," and the most devotional of all eucharistic hymns; Saint Bernard of
Menthon going with his followers to found the hos-

pice at the top of the Alpine Pass of the Grand Saint Bernard, where the monks, with their dogs, saved so many poor travellers lost in the winter's snows; Thomas a Kempis writing his "Imitation of Christ," which next to the Bible has reached more souls than any other book; Abelard, the philosopher and schoolman, whose works may have been unorthodox, but whose unique romance with Heloise and his subsequent life as a Monk of Cluny, make him ever interesting; the solemn chanting of the Divine Offices in many a Monastic chapel, heard only by God; "Religious" going forth as missionary Monks to convert the heathen in many a distant clime—one might go on and on and never find exhausted the romance of the "Religious" and their record of mighty works done for God. And what a splendid thing it would be if many of those who have returned from the war, trying hard to forget the sights and experiences of that conflict, could be drawn to the Monastic Life, perhaps a vicarious sacrifice for a sinning world.

XVIII

CONCERNING BISHOPS

IN A BOOK on the Sacred Ministry, one could hardly omit a few thoughts on the highest of the three Orders, that of Bishops. That which is here set forth, however, is not venturing to give counsel to the members of the Episcopate, but rather to call to mind, for the benefit of Clergy and Laity alike, some things which should always be remembered about the Right Reverend Fathers in God.

As with the Ordination of a Priest, so with the Consecration of a Bishop, there must be proper "matter," "form" and "intention." As these are assured, the validity of the Orders of the Anglican Church is not a matter of opinion, but a matter of fact. Consequently, each Bishop of the Church is a successor of the Apostles, consecrated to his office by other Bishops, all of whom continue the Apostolic Succession. And this Episcopate, to which he is consecrated, is not only for the *"well-being"* of the Church, but also for the *"being"* of the Church, the office of a Bishop being a necessity to the Holy Catholic Church, for it has been well said: *"Where there is the Bishop, there is the Church."* There can be no valid Orders except they be conferred by the Bishops, who must derive their powers from the past through the Apostolic Succession.

The office and work of a Bishop has been defined as that of Consecrating, Ordaining and Blessing in the name of Christ and the Church. The Bishop is also to safeguard the doctrine, discipline and worship of the Church. Unfortunately in the Anglican Communion, the Bishop of a Diocese has not always been a reliable authority, for often his private views and opinions, his likes and dislikes, have been substituted for that which the Church holds and sets forth. For it must always be remembered by Bishops as by others, that the Church's teaching and tradition and not private opinion is to prevail. As the Anglican Communion is a part of the True Church she rightly inherits all those blessings and privileges which are of the whole Catholic Church, in faith or practice. That which is the tradition of the whole is the tradition of the part, unless definitely denied in her formularies.

The proportion of Bishops to Priests in the past was far greater than it is now. Whether or not the Church would be benefitted by more Bishops is a question. Some opinions favour this, divided, however, as to whether it would be better to have small Dioceses with one Bishop, or large Dioceses with a Diocesan assisted by Co-adjutors and Suffragans. This hardly comes within the scope of this book.

The names of many Bishops throughout the two thousand years of Church History have come down to us as great Saints, great Scholars, great Missionaries. And today, the Episcopate, for all the changed times and changed conditions, rightly boasts of many distinguished names of Godly learning and of Godly life.

The Bishop really has a very difficult part to play. His Office is one of high honour but also one of great responsibility. To maintain it upon a high spiritual plane, in the face of the routine business which is his to transact, needs constant recourse to all of the aids of the religious life; prayer, mass and sacrament. If he can frequently offer the Sacrifice of the Altar, and seek Divine guidance in all the difficult problems which may arise, he will prove to be no unworthy Bishop, but will be in very truth a "Right Reverend *Father* in God," who has the welfare of every Priest and every Parish in his Diocese written in his heart. Then it will be no mere praise or flattery or lip service, but real affection and respect when he is referred to as "Our beloved Bishop." The time has gone by when a Bishop thought that his greatest assets were a fine presence and a sonorous voice, and when he assumed the grand air, such as a slangy boy described as "that of the Big Boss"!

The Bishop often finds in his Diocese that those who are best fitted financially to help the work are the least spiritually minded or the least religiously inclined. To them the Church is more a place for personal prominence and influence than the mystical Body of Christ, which is to be "the Preserver of Truth, the Dispenser of Grace and the Guide in Morals." And as a consequence, the Bishop comes to know that here is a force which may easily become an opposition. Sometimes he senses how these persons are trying to make their position and power influence him. Alas! Not seldom are our Right Reverend Fathers in God found following the wishes of these worldly-minded members instead of seeking to maintain the standards that appeal to the spiritually and religiously inclined! At Consecration a Bishop promised *"with all faithful diligence to banish and drive away from the Church all erroneous and strange doctrine contrary to God's Word"; and both privately and openly to call upon and encourage others to the same."* Yet occasionally in some dioceses, Bishops have allowed to flourish teachings close to "false doctrine, heresy and schism," with no reproof, rebuke or prohibition. Consequently, it is no unusual thing to find in some Parishes the denial of the Virgin Birth, attacks upon the integrity of the Incarnation or the Resurrection of Our Lord, irreverent teachings regarding the Blessed Sacrament, admitting to Holy Communion the unconfirmed or those who have no idea of belonging to the Church, all of which is absolutely contrary to the doctrine, discipline and worship of the Church, as set forth in the Book of Common Prayer.

And this has led to the sad picture: one Parish may deny some of the most important articles of the Creed, and never a word of condemnation from the Diocesan, and another is under a cloud of Episcopal disapproval, because it gives special honour to Christ in the Blessed Sacrament and has Confession and Benediction! So that it is a true joy to the faithful to turn to those Bishops and those Dioceses where the Faith is kept inviolate and all godly practices that help in the spiritual life are approved and commended, whether or not they appeal to the individual views or preferences of the Right Reverend Father in God.

The relations of a Rector or Parish Priest with the Bishop should be happy ones and undoubtedly may be if there is shown mutual courtesy and consideration. The Priest naturally values his friendship with his Bishop, appreciates his visitation to his Parish and respects his high office, but he rightly expects him to be a true "Father in God," and not a domineering Church official on the warpath. The writer, in a somewhat long ministry, has always been most fortunate in having had the most friendly relations with six different Bishops of varying religious views who were his Diocesans. All of them recognized his right to run his Parish as he deemed proper if according to the accepted faith and practice of the Church. These were true and godly Bishops!

A good Bishop therefore recognizes that not his will or personal preferences are to decide what is right or proper, but rather the traditional teaching and practice of the Church and the Law of the Church, where it has been defined. He also remembers at a Visitation that the character and conduct of the Service is not his responsibility, but that of the Rector, to whose "use," as a matter of courtesy, he should be glad to conform. As a Bishop of all kinds of Churchmen, he should be expected so far as possible to adapt himself to the various kinds of Services, having familiarized himself with all kinds of Rites and Ceremonies allowed by the Church. Thus, in a Parish where everything is very simple, he would probably wear his rochet and chimere (generally called "the Bishop's Robes"!), but in a different kind of Church, he would wear Cope and Mitre or other customary Episcopal Vestments.

The Bishop will find himself treated with the greatest respect (especially if he does not take himself too seriously and assume the "grand air"). He will generally find that the Parish Priest has gone to considerable pains to teach the people of the honour accruing to his high office, and if meeting the Bishop to curtsey or give a low bow and even kiss the Episcopal Ring.

In most walks of life, those in high place try to familiarize themselves with all the various things associated with their position. Although not called upon, they wish to be able to discharge any duty that might arise or direct someone how to perform it. Some Bishops, however, who have been chosen from the "Low Church" or "Protestant" part of the Church, although knowing that they must be the "Spiritual Father in God" to all types of Churchmen, never take the pains to understand or to be able to follow the ritual and ceremonial in our "Catholic Parishes," for all some of them are most important parts of the whole. One would think that a Bishop, no matter what are his private views and preferences, would like to be conversant with all that is done and not be like a fish out of the water, totally ignorant as to what the ceremonial means or how to conform. Surely such an attitude neither makes for the exaltation of the Bishop nor for the respect that the Clergy and people would like to give him. And when, as in rare instances, the Right Reverend Father in God, to show his dislike for all that he has never taken the trouble to understand, irreverently flaunts these things, he fails as a Spiritual Father and he loses the approval and affection of the people. In a *right* sense, a

Bishop should be *"all things to all men,"* a *Father to all* of his Diocese, able to conform to whatever kind of proper Service he finds in the various parishes. The Clergy and the Congregation *wish* to love, respect and admire their Right Reverend Fathers in God, but they desire that they be *worthy* of such honour and affection. Let them be real leaders, free from pride and prejudice, and they will have a loving and loyal following. Let them be "godly and learned men," as they were presented for Consecration, and they will have the respect and reverence of all. Let them remember and fulfil their vows and promises (as a Priest should ever remember and fulfil his) and they will not fail in their high office but will have their names writ large amongst those who have ranked as truly Right Reverend Fathers in God.

XIX

MARRIED AND UNMARRIED CLERGY

Sooner or later in the study of the Sacred Ministry comes the consideration of the possible marriage or celibacy of the Clergy. Should they be married or single? Is there any Divine Revelation on the subject? Is there any rule or regulation that governs the matter? Is there any general usage that obtains? Or is a Priest free to do as he pleases, to marry if he so wishes, to remain single if he thinks best, or to take the vows of celibacy. A few words on the subject may clear up matters and show the individual freedom in the Anglican Communion.

The celibacy or marriage of the Clergy is not a matter of Divine Law. They have been regulated according to the discipline of the Church, which has varied in different ages. Some of the Apostles were married, some were not. Beginning almost with the Apostolic Age, opinions varied on the subject and there arose a conflict, continued throughout the centuries between those who wished celibacy to be enforced and those who approved liberty as to marriage. This controversy, with its consequent rules, regulations, permissions and changes, may here be passed over.

Speaking generally, today the Roman Catholic Church requires the Celibacy of the Clergy (excepting in the case of the "Uniates," who have been accorded a special dispensation), the Holy Orthodox Eastern Church insists upon the marriage of the Parish Priests (although Bishops must be monks or widowers) and the Anglican Communion allows perfect freedom in the matter. The decision is left to the conscience of the Clergy, as to whether God can best be served by a man in the celibate or married life. And while for years it seemed to be assumed that when an Anglican Priest married, it would be before Ordination, apparently this restriction no longer obtains. It can hardly be denied that this freedom in respect to marriage has worked most advantageously in the Anglican Communion, where the same sanctity of life and consecration of talents is seen alike amongst the married and the unmarried.

From many practical points of view, it seems to be a general opinion, that in small parishes, especially in the country and in the suburbs, the married Clergy seem best adapted for the work, while in great city Churches, especially in the poorer districts, and in the foreign missionary field, the celibate or unmarried Clergy should be chosen, for there is an inspiration in a group of Priests living and working together in a common centre.

There is one thing, however, that a Priest should remember if married. When he takes unto himself a partner, she is united to him in Holy Matrimony, but she is not entering Holy Orders! It is both ridiculous and scandalous to see, as is sometimes the case, the wife of a Priest intruding in the affairs of the Parish and apparently trying to run things, either directly through her own interference or indirectly by constraining her husband to carry out her wishes. If a Priest is married, he should see that his wife always conducts herself as *one of the congregation* and not as a favoured person. By never being the head of any guild or society, she avoids rivalry, jealousy and escapes both the criticism or commendation which the Priest might have to give. In fact, it is often better for the wife of a married Priest not to engage in any Church work in his Parish, but to confine her efforts to making his home one of peace, joy and inspiration and devote her outside labours to diocesan work.

Many Parishes, in considering the matter of calling a Rector and deciding upon the advisability of choosing a married or unmarried Priest, have sometimes come to be actuated by rather unworthy motives. For instead of weighing which one can do the most effective work in the religious and spiritual life of the people, they only count the cost and so come to be influenced by the thought of how cheaply they can secure the services of a Priest. One may like to think that this is not true but there is no gainsaying the facts. And while there may be some excuse in a Parish of very little means, as a rule, it is an unworthy procedure and does not work out for the Church's good.

It is not the intention here to advocate the cause of either the married or the unmarried Clergy. Both can stand on their records and accomplishments for the cause of God, and lacking any Divine Law on the subject, the proper position would seem that of approving both states of life in the Sacred Priesthood.

XX

THE CONDUCT OF THE CLERGY

THE CHURCH rightly expects of her lay members high ideals and standards and a life conformable to the same. There is no puritanical prohibition of innocent enjoyments, taken in moderation, such as society, the dance, the stage, the opera, the playing of cards, the indulgence in sports, the use of wines and the like. All of these things are permitted and approved if they do not interfere with one's religious or temporal duties, are not contrary to good manners and good morals, and are not regarded in an hedonistic way, making pleasure the main object of life.

Yet while *"all things are lawful, all things are not expedient,"* as applied to the Clergy. The world, whether religious or irreligious, expects the conduct of a Priest to be superior to that which obtains in ordinary pursuits. He is supposed not only to practice that which he preaches, but also to make this preaching and practice an inspiration to all. In a way, he is always on duty, always on parade, always in the public eye. That which he is, or does, or says is judged critically. Consequently, he will be a help or a hindrance to others by the way his conduct measures up to the expected ideal or standard. This is why, at Ordination, he is solemnly asked,

"Will you be diligent to frame and fashion your ownselves, and your families, according to the doctrine of Christ and to make both yourselves and them, as much as in you lieth, wholesome examples and patterns to the flock of Christ," to which counsel he gives assent in the words: *"I will apply myself thereto, the Lord being my Helper."* This question and answer constitute a counsel, obligation and promise that the Priest should always remember and model his life accordingly.

In the fulfillment of his Ordination Vows, the Priest must give up some things, perfectly innocent in themselves, but detrimental to the regard in which his Sacred Office should be held. He, like others, needs times of relaxation and recreation, but they should be in such moderation that his priestly duties and responsibilities are never interfered with, but should ever stand forth as the main occupations of his life. He may rightly expect a vacation from time to time but it seems a mistake for the Clergy regularly to "take a whole day off weekly," as is the custom of some. For it gives the impression that their cares are few, that they do not regard their responsibilities very seriously and are rather "play-boys." And that hurts both them and the Church.

Experience and observation have taught that as a rule, frequenting of clubs, or playing cards should be avoided, drinking parties should never be attended and no show or place of amusement should be visited that is in the slightest way open to criticism. It should be the invariable custom of a Priest to refuse to gamble, to bet, or to play for money. Often the Clergy have lost the respect of the community and have injured their influence by doing these things. Particularly is this so in the use of stimulants. The Church does not constrain to "total abstinence," but it most surely counsels "*let your moderation be known unto all men*," and if one does occasionally "drink of the cup that cheers," it cautions as to "where," "when," and "with whom." Frequently members of the Laity who invite the Clergy to drink with them are most caustic in their criticism of them and severe in their condemnation behind their backs. Perhaps it is better for "the Man of God" to refrain entirely or else make exceptions only on rare occasions.

A fallacy, held by some of the Clergy, is that their popularity and influence with the Laity is increased when they are most informal, when they are "good mixers," and when they dress like laymen! Sometimes "Solomon in all his glory" was not arrayed as one of these! Why, however, a plaid suit and a red cravat, or a little "cussing," or the drinking of a cocktail, should be considered a help in winning the laymen to the Kingdom of Heaven, passes comprehension! As a matter of fact, the contrary seems to be the case. Some of the laity wonder just why a Priest does not wish to wear his clericals, which are his uniform! Others speculate as to whether he is not "up to some mischief," the doing something or the going somewhere that would be a reflection upon his Sacred Office. It is certainly wiser to avoid the appearance of evil. It is certainly better to dress as a Priest and follow the old tradition of being smooth shaven, or having a beard, which custom seems to have met with genuine approval.

There is a good story, very old, for it goes back to the days of horses, of an English Bishop, who called to task a Curate with rather "sporty tastes" and who had caused scandal by driving a tandem, innocent as this seems today. The Curate could not see the harm, he objected to the criticism, he resented the counsel and finally said to the Bishop: "What difference is there in your driving a *pair* of horses and my driving a *tandem?*" The Bishop replied, "I will show you." So, putting his hands together as one does in prayer, he said: "This shows the way I drive"; then, putting one hand in front of the other, with the thumb at his nose, "This is the way you drive!" So, things innocent in themselves, have often to be avoided because of the criticism they invoke, even if often the criticism is foolish.

Another danger to the Clergy is that of too intimate association with the other sex, in the Church and in Society. Often perfectly innocent relations compromise a Priest. In parochial work, the Priest constantly comes in contact with the women of the Parish, meets them at the Guilds, directs them in certain duties, hears matters of a somewhat confidential nature and comes to know many of them well. It needs tact and wisdom to be smiling, approachable, and companionable, yet always careful to maintain a certain reserve and formality, always to make the relations those of friendship between a Priest and his people. And in Penance, in the hearing of Confessions, this reserve and formality are most requisite, so that the personal or individual character is forgotten and only that of the Priest and Penitent obtain.

In his conduct therefore, the Priest must ever remember that he is one set apart, called to this Office of the Sacred Ministry. In his vocation *"the*

Cure of Souls" he must be one whose life *"is hid with Christ in God,"* by word and example trying to bring Souls to God and God to Souls, instilling in them the love and fear of God and the keeping of God's Commandments. Not through great gifts nor marked talents, nor notable achievements, helpful as they are, but through a pleasing personality, a godly character and right conduct, *"without fear and without reproach,"* will he make his ministry redound for the Glory of God, the honour of Christ and the winning of Souls for the Kingdom of Heaven.

On vacation, the Clergy, while laying aside for awhile their responsibilities, and rightly seeking suitable rest, relaxation and recreation, must remember that they *are not on vacation from their religion.* Their own, spiritual life must be ministered to as much on holiday as at work and their daily devotions are not to cease because away from Church. Many Priests never have the chance or the money for a real vacation. If, however, they do have, this time should be so wisely used, that amidst the pleasures of the holiday, the Priest is being refreshed in mind and body, resolved to be still more faithful and devoted to his work, upon his return. Fresh air and exercise cannot be too highly commended. Golf and tennis and swimming are great aids, for as a man improves physically, he grows better mentally and spiritually.

Abroad, the Clergy have been amongst the greatest climbers in the Alps, the mountains apparently always attracting the *"Man of God."* Truly, as the Psalmist says, *"The mountains shall bring peace,"* *"I will look unto the hills from whence cometh my help."* In those sunlit realms of ice and snow, forest and meadow, with marvelous views of soaring summits and glistening glaciers, perhaps roseate in the Alpine glow, the soul seems very close to God, for *"the works of nature are the footprints of the Creator,"* and there comes many a beautiful thought or pious resolution that will bear fruit at home. It may be interesting to note that many of the Clergy who have been distinguished mountaineers climbed dressed as Priests or at least retained their clerical collar and rabat.

It is absolutely essential to the effective work of a Priest that he be a man of the highest moral character. He may be married or unmarried, living according to the estate he has chosen, but he must ever follow the law of chastity. In thought, word or deed he should resist all temptations to impurity of any kind whatsoever. *"Blessed are the pure in heart, for they shall see God"* could be paraphrased: "Blessed are those of the Sacred Ministry who are pure in thought, word and deed for they will ever inspire those about them to cultivate the beauty of holiness."

Sometimes on vacation, a Priest meets people who are seeking information on many religious matters and who are desirous of godly counsel. They may have been diffident about asking on these subjects in their own Parishes or may have felt, rightly or wrongly, that their own Clergy were rather unapproachable. Here then is an opportunity for helping the work of the Church and the Priest on vacation should rejoice at the chance.

Often, too, a Priest may be taking his holiday where perhaps the Church he attends is a chapel or mission open only in the summer. He can generally arrange with the Priest in charge to say Mass from time to time, even daily in places and very often he may be asked to preach. All of this should be welcomed, for a vacation does not mean a holiday from the practice of his religion, but rather a temporary escape from the responsibilities of his home work and the seeking for change and rest. And if the vacation includes travel, there will be many a memory laid up from which to draw lessons upon his return. Let every Priest take a vacation when possible, but always let him remember that he is a Priest. And let the holiday, when over, see him back home more fully surrendered to his chosen calling, seeing Christ in every soul and loving to minister for the glory of God and the good of mankind. Truly Saint Augustine said: *"First give thyself to God, then to the work God gives thee to do."*

XXI

FUNERALS AND CHURCHYARDS

ONE OF THE DUTIES of a Priest is to minister the last offices of the dead. This would be a very sad privilege if it were not for the Christian belief in the Resurrection and the knowledge that earthly death is but the entrance into that larger and more wonderful life beyond the veil.

A Parish Priest or Rector becomes very much attached to those to whom he ministers, an affection or friendship which deepens as the years roll by in one "cure." Consequently, the passing of those so enshrined in his heart is a personal sorrow as well as a parochial loss. Yet, as with a doctor in the loss of a patient, so with the Priest in the loss of a parishioner: he comes to accept it as the inevitable, a little chapter in the journey of life and he does his utmost to discharge his last duties to the dear departed.

The last rites of the dead should be a Requiem Mass, the offering up of the holy Sacrifice of the Altar that the soul of the dear departed *"may rest in peace and that light perpetual may shine upon him,"* as goes the solemn antiphon. This has been the Church's custom for centuries. No matter how hard it may be for the Clergy in a large Parish, where there are many funerals, *a Requiem Mass should be the regular rule*. This is really the right way to remember the dead, for the supplementary Service in the Prayer Book, called *"The Order for the Burial of the Dead,"* originally presupposed a Mass, and itself has more relation to the comfort of the living than to the repose of the Soul of the dear departed. Protestant bodies have lost this privilege of offering up the Mass or Communion for the dead. There is no excuse, however, for Anglicans to follow them and be content with the mere Burial Office and so deprive the dead of Our Lord's Own Service said or sung for them, pleading Christ's Passion and Death for those who *"die in the Lord."*

A Requiem Mass omits certain parts, especially the Creed (since faith is lost in sight) and the Gloria in Excelsis (as unsuitable to such a Service). What are called the "propers" are specially applicable to the dead. The great thought that runs through the whole Requiem Mass (and which is also in the Form for the Absolution of the Body, which follows) is that of the Antiphon: *"Rest eternal grant to them, O Lord, and let light perpetual shine upon them."* A very good way is to read the short Burial Office at the house on the evening before and in the morning to carry the body into the Church for a Solemn Mass of Requiem, followed by the Absolution.

The Clergy will be remiss if they do not, from time to time, instruct their people in the proper care of the dead. This teaching largely affects the attitude of the living. It must be the observation and experience of many, that generally speaking, Protestants seem to be fearful of the dead, while Catholics (in which are included all properly instructed Anglicans) reverence the bodies of the dear departed and so not dread to be with them. Consequently, they follow the devout custom of the Church for centuries: to have the body laid out in some room of the house, with Crucifix or Cross and Candles, where at certain times or continuously prayers are said for the repose of the Soul. And it would seem that those who love their dead or who have lost those close to them would show their affection or respect by wearing black, which is both fitting and seemly. One of the disturbing signs of today is the growing lack of respect for the dead, the short and hurried funerals, the disregard of the conventional outward signs of mourning and the attempt to write "finis" to the memory.

It is not out of place here to commend to everyone that splendid work of "The Guild of All Souls," and to hope that all will wish to be members of it. It teaches the proper care of the dead, it remembers the dear departed, and it provides poor parishes and missions with the means properly to celebrate Masses of Requiem.

The Church rarely has Sermons at a funeral, except in the case of one specially distinguished or when specially asked. A Sermon seems to detract from the solemnity of the occasion, unnecessarily lengthens the Service and adds nothing to the estimation in which the dead is held. Generally speaking, one's good works are more or less known and the really Christian man or woman would not wish to be publicly extolled for living a good life.

Apropos of a Sermon at a funeral, reminds the Author of a clerical friend of his, who, once connected with the City Mission, was asked to officiate at a burial up in the country. Arriving at the Church, while he was vesting, he was asked if he would kindly make an address over the dead. He said it was not customary with the "Episcopal Church," but consented to do so. After the Service, when he had preached this sermon and was again in the Sacristy, he asked if his address had pleased them. One may picture his chagrin when he was told: "Father, it was meant well; all that you said about *his* 'character' and *his* 'good works' and the 'regard in which *he* was held by the community,' but you see the deceased *was a young woman!*"

The Author has sung many a Requiem Mass, for in his Parish for years there has rarely been a funeral that did not have a Mass. It has always been a very solemn and beautiful Service and oftentimes it has been said that the sadness of it all was forgotten in the feeling that it was like reverently giving back to God one made *"in His image and after His Likeness,"* who dying in a state of grace, *"doth rest from his labours where his works do follow him."*

It has always been a hallowed custom of the Church to have the bodies of the dead rest in consecrated ground which is often called "God's Acre." When the burial takes place in a Churchyard connected with some Parish, one is sure that the ground has been blessed and properly set apart for this purpose. As, however, there are many cemeteries not belonging to the Church, which have never been consecrated, the Priest having a burial there in one of them should be sure to bless the grave before the body is put into its final resting place. This may seem a very little and unimportant matter to some, but to the reverent minded, who know the hallowed use of centuries, it is most important and most desirable.

Frequently, the Clergy are consulted by members of the family of the deceased as to the kind of stone to place at the grave and the kind of inscription to be used. While this is a matter that does not really directly concern the Clergy, nevertheless, when asked, they should be able to advise that which seems most fitting. Many will think that nothing is better than a marble slab placed over a vaulted tomb. Or if a grass or ivy covered grave is to be had, then a head-stone and footstone, or perhaps a Latin Cross. The dreadful monstrosities once in vogue, running any-where from a classical temple to a weeping virgin, are not sought after nowadays! As to inscriptions, the more general they are, the better. One very religious one, that enshrines the thought of the future, is some-what as follows according to ancient and traditional use: In the Hope of a Glorious Resurrection, Here Entered into Life ————. followed by a text, as for example, *"Blessed are the pure in heart, for they shall see God,"* or *"They do rest from their labours and their works do follow them,"* or *"The Eternal God is thy refuge and underneath are the Everlasting Arms."*

It is hoped that it will not be unseemly to refer to the other foolish kind of an inscription by recalling the old story of Bishop Potter. One of his clergy called upon him saying he was in great trouble. A year ago he had lost his wife. Now he was to marry again. The Bishop did not know whether to console or congratulate! "But what is the trouble you are in?" "Well, you see, Bishop, on my wife's tomb I had inscribed 'My light has gone out.'" "Oh," said Bishop Potter, "don't worry about that; just add the words, 'I have struck another match!'"

XXII

OF LESSER THINGS

At first, it may seem trivial and unimportant to care how the Clergy are addressed. Upon consideration, however, one realizes that not only should the usual laws of courtesy obtain, but also that the mode of address should be such as befits the high office of the Sacred Ministry.

In addressing certain persons in high position, there is an accepted and approved use, such as "His Excellency, the President," "His Grace, the Archbishop," "His Honor, the Mayor," and in speaking to them, one says "Your Excellency" or "Your Grace" or "Your Honor." According to this usage, it would be proper to refer to a Priest as "His Reverence" and speak to him as "Your Reverence." This, however, is very rarely done, except perhaps "in the oulde counthree" where "His Riverence" is quite usual.

Addressing the Clergy properly in letters and conversation is really a matter of some importance, for it is a mark of good manners and good usage. It would seem fitting that the address would have some reference to the profession. A commander of a ship is called "Captain" and a physician is spoken to as "Doctor." Neither of these is addressed "Mister." Nor should a Priest be called "Mister." The natural and proper name should be "Father," for this shows his spiritual relationship to his people and serves to remind him of his responsibilities. That this is the custom in the Roman Catholic body is an argument for, not against, its use, for nowhere is found a more respectful and affectionate attitude towards the Clergy than in that Communion. Some of the Anglican Priests affect to dislike the title, but their sincerity may be questioned, for it is very "taking" to hear that friendly greeting from every one, even the little children, "Good morning, Father." It is difficult to see what valid objection there could be to this mode of address.

In France, it is customary to speak to and of the Clergy as "Père," "Monsieur le Curé," and "Monsieur," but it should be noted that "Monsieur" is not the equivalent of "Mister."

The address should not be associated with any kind of Churchmanship. As was said at the start, it should refer to the Sacred Office. "Mister" is a meaningless title, "Doctor" an academic name, and "Reverend" an inexcusable crudity, unworthy of refined use.

While on the subject of the proper way in which to address the Clergy, a word may be said about the correct usage in referring to their parishes when named after Saints. For recently, there has crept in a most corrupt abbreviation, the using of the letter "S" for Saint. This has doubtless been done thoughtlessly, for everyone doubtless knows that in English, "St." is the abbreviation for "Saint," as in French likewise, where "St." or "Ste." are used respectively for the masculine or feminine. And while occasionally "Saint" is abbreviated in the Prayer Book, it is always by "St." Why should one abbreviate an English word by an Italian use? For that is what "S" is, as for instance "Santa Maria" or "San Clemente" have the word for "Saint," that is the Italian "San" or "Santa," signified by "S." If the Anglican Communion was Italian, and her Churches were under Italian names, all well and good, but since it is the English speaking part of the Holy Catholic Church and her places of worship bear English names, the only good and correct way is to follow the proper use and abbreviate "Saint" as "St."

Considerable confusion comes from the possession of a degree. Many do not realize that degrees, whether received "in course" or "honoris causa" are academic. Some may be conferred alike on the Laity and the Clergy, such as LL.D., D.C.L. Those who receive what may be called lesser degrees, like Ph.D., are not generally addressed as "Doctor." The two really "ecclesiastical" degrees that give the possessor the privilege of being spoken of as "Doctor," if he so wishes, are D.D. and S.T.D.

And one should always remember that those in the Sacred Ministry should never be referred to as "the Minister" or "our Minister." For when ordained they were not made "Ministers of the Gospel" (which are sectarians) but "Priests of the Church"

XXIII

AN AFTERWORD

IN WRITING this little book upon the LIGHTS AND SHADOWS OF THE SACRED MINISTRY, the Author has not presumed to do more than to set forth certain thoughts and teaching that may be helpful, with God's blessing, to all who read. Perhaps a long ministry of almost fifty years may through prayer and sacraments, reading and experience, enable one to be of some spiritual help and inspiration to those who read. This is the writer's humble endeavour.

It is hoped the foregoing chapters have clearly set forth that above all the Priest must be, in the words of the Scripture, "a Man of God," a good man, of high character. While all of the ministerial acts of a Priest are valid, notwithstanding his possible unworthiness, the influence of a holy life and godly character is beyond estimate. To be a man of prayer, to be spiritually minded, to practice that which he preaches, to be full of the love and fear of God, to be possessed of a never-failing charity, to have a sincere longing for Souls, to love the Service and Worship of God, to be ever mindful of his ministry, to be thoroughly surrendered and consecrated to God will win more Souls for the Kingdom of Heaven than anything else.

Even the most careless and worldly have a respect for goodness. And when they see a Priest, reflecting the life of Christ in his own life, he will be as a magnet drawing people to God! Example ever speaks louder than words. Given a real "Man of God," devoted to the Master, and full of good works, and all sorts and conditions of men will be found drawn to God by the inspiration of His humble Servant.

Such Clergy are needed today as never before. One does not like to blame the evils of the day upon the Church and the Clergy. As has been well said, "Christianity has not failed. Only it has not been practiced." Yet while the Church and the Clergy cannot in fairness be made responsible for the woeful lack of religion today, in some measure at least they have contributed to this condition inasmuch as the Church has often spoken with uncertain voice and the Clergy have not been the inspiring examples that they should have been. The Church will have to arise in her might and her Clergy return to Apostolic purity and fervour again to make religion the constraining power in the world today.

The world is threatened today as never before. All kinds of evil abound. The very foundations of society are shaken. Crime, corruption and vice are rampant. All walks of life, high and low, show a terrible declination from former accepted ideals and standards. Generations have grown up without any faith or discipline. The youth is rebellious against all authority. The home life has largely gone. Money and pleasure rule the day. Communism and Marxism are attacking the very foundations of the Christian Religion. Many of the Churches show diminishing congregations. The faith of our fathers is neglected, scoffed at or abandoned. Civilization is pursuing a path that has well been said, unless arrested, will destroy itself. The only cure, *the only salvation is religion*, real religion, the truth Faith, the revelation of God in Christ, the keeping of the Ten Commandments, the following of the Golden Rule, the praise, worship and service of Almighty God, the putting into being the practice of religion as Our Blessed Lord has given the same, *"to do justly, to love mercy, and to walk humbly with God." Only religion can save the world!*

So the Church needs Priests, godly Priests, learned Priests, full of the love of God, full of devotion to Christ, full of loyalty to the Church, hungering and thirsting for the things of God, longing for Souls to be shepherded into the True Church, there faithfully to practice their religion and to show forth that religion in godly living, in brotherly love.

Here then is the opportunity. Here is the vineyard. Here the fields are ripe for harvest. Here the labourers are needed for the new Crusade, the bringing of Christ and the Church back to a wicked and gainsaying world, to give men the True Religion. The Church calls all of us, those of us already ordained, those in preparation for the Sacred Ministry, those who may have vocation but have never thought of it, to be good and holy disciplined and sacrificing Priests, true Men of God, real examples to the flock of Christ, saving our own souls in the saving of others, witnessing to the Faith we hold by preaching and living it before the world. *"Who then is willing to consecrate his services this day unto the Lord!"*